Poetry

JOSÉ GARCIA VILLA'S
PHILOSOPHY OF POETRY

# Poetry is

Edited by Robert L King

ATENEO DE MANILA UNIVERSITY PRESS

ATENEO DE MANILA UNIVERSITY PRESS

Bellarmine Hall, Katipunan Avenue
Loyola Heights, Quezon City
P.O. Box 154, 1099 Manila, Philippines
Tel.: (632) 426-59-84 / Fax (632) 426-59-09
E-mail: unipress@admu.edu.ph
Website: www.ateneopress.org



Book and cover design by Ali Figueroa



THE NATIONAL LIBRARY OF THE PHILIPPINES CIP DATA

Recommended entry:

Poetry is : Jose Garcia Villa's philosophy of poetry / edited by Robert L. King. -- Quezon City : Ateneo de Manila University Press, [c2015].

xxii, 174 pages ; 22.86 cm.

ISBN 978-971-550-717-2

1. Poetry -- Philosophy. 2. Poetics. 3. Poetry -- Grammar. 4. Poetry -- Study and teaching. I. King, Robert L.

808.1 PN1031 2015 P420150292

For JOSÉ

Poet, Mentor, Friend, Surrogate Father

When you leave, I will lose nothing
    and everything! )for nothing worth losing
I had before, and

When you're gone, I will have nothing
    and everything! )for the everything
you were you

Still will remain, as the something,
    the very thing, your nothingness has
left behind.

# CONTENTS

ACKNOWLEDGMENTS ix

INTRODUCTION xi

EDITOR'S NOTE xix

POETRY IS

1 In Poetry, What You Don't Know Can Hurt You 1

2 Poetry is Not Self Expression 8

3 What is Poetry? 10

4 Differences Between Poetry and Prose 17

5 Magic and Genesis in Poetry 19

6 The Kinetics of Poetry 24

7 Language 26

8 Rhythm in Poetry 30

9 Organizational Differences Between Poetry and Prose 32

10 Borderline Cases 42

11 Free Verse 45

12 Verse and Lyricism 50

13 Purity in Poetry 55

14 Great Poetry 68

15 Wrapping Up on Poetry's "Internals" 75
16 Poetic Language 80
17 Introduction to Poetic Technique 85
18 The Inception of the Poem 93
19 Propulsion of the First Line into a Poem 104
20 The Musical Situation 109
21 The Verbal Situation 115
22 The Semantic Situation 120
23 The Craft of Versification 124
24 Abstraction in Poetry 143
25 Resolution and Last Line 148
Villa's Postscript 155

**EDITOR'S EPILOGUE** **159**
**APPENDIX ON ADAPTATIONS** **163**
**BIBLIOGRAPHY** **168**
**INDEX** **170**

# ACKNOWLEDGMENTS

I wish to express my profound gratitude to John Edwin Cowen, the Literary Trustee of the Estate of José Garcia Villa, for his faithful service as such, without which this book would not have been possible. Collecting and preserving the Villa papers now residing in the Houghton Library Collection at Harvard University that serve as the principal source material for this book was a prodigious task, and John went beyond by patiently supervising the scanning of Villa's first three binders of lecture materials into digital form, enabling this Editor to commence his work even before these papers found their way to Harvard. I also wish to thank Leslie Morris of the Houghton Library and her very professional staff for facilitating my review of the remaining papers during my lengthy visit to the Library in 2009.

I must also gratefully record my indebtedness to John and to Mort Malkin, another long-time José loyalist, for their invaluable comments and suggestions regarding my manuscript and for their sophisticated proofreading of same, which on occasion reacquainted me with my dog-eared copies of Fowler's *A Dictionary of Modern English Usage*, first and second editions.

I would like to thank John Felstiner, Professor Emeritus of English, Stanford University, for reviewing my materials and engaging in a spirited discussion with me about our respective views of what poetry is, including the variances in our views which were far less than our agreements. His suggestions for revision greatly enhanced the text of this book and, I am sure, made it more palatable to those poetry readers he referred to as "groomed lately"—a characterization that describes neither of us as we are roughly of the same age.

Last but not least, I wish to acknowledge the support from my two "muses," Dr. Ruth Bolton and Alice Palmer Thomas, in the laborious task of finding a publisher who these days will have anything to do with poetry and poetics.

Sadly, John Edwin Cowen passed away on August 23, 2012. With his death, responsibility for Villa's Literary Estate passed to the Executor of Villa's Last Will and Testament, his youngest son, Lance Christian Villa.

In the above picture taken November 9, 1948 at the Gotham Book Mart in New York City, José Garcia Villa (standing in the back to the left of the ladder) was keeping company with some of the most important poets, authors and critics of the 1940s. Dame Edith Sitwell and her brother Osbert are seated in the center to the left of Villa. On Villa's right are W. H. Auden (seated on the ladder) and, moving clockwise around the Sitwells, Elizabeth Bishop, Marianne Moore, Delmore Schwartz, Randall Jarrell, Charles Henri Ford (seated, cross-legged, on the floor), William Rose Benet, Stephen Spender, Marya Zaturenska, Horace Gregory, Tennessee Williams, Richard Eberhart, and Gore Vidal. (Getty Images)

# INTRODUCTION

In this era, what makes for poetry remains open to question, yet more vital than ever. How does poetry differ from prose? What constitutes and qualifies as free verse and is it poetry? Does a prosaic "poem," even one that truly touches us but lacks artistic form, truly qualify as poetry? Is poetry whatever a reader or writer wants it to be—as Humpty Dumpty tells Alice: "When *I* use a word, it means just what I choose it to mean—neither more nor less." Her response is prophetic: "The question is whether you *can* make words mean so many different things."[1]

This book revives the views of José Garcia Villa (1908–1997), now lesser-known but a striking presence in the mid-20th century. Among his friends and admirers were E. E. Cummings, Edith Sitwell, Robert Frost, Dylan Thomas and Marianne Moore. In the mid-1950s, Villa turned from writing poems to the philosophy of poetry, explaining the making and makings of poems as a serious art, and what they can and cannot do. For Villa, a piece of poetry that becomes a poem is susceptible to precise definition and is not open to various interpretations widely attributed to poetry.

Aided by a Bollingen Foundation Fellowship in 1951 to 1953 and a Rockefeller Foundation Fellowship in 1963, Villa developed a *theory of poetry* that is the subject of this book, and taught two poetry workshops at New York City College from 1952 to 1960 and at The New School for Social Research from 1964 to 1973. The first workshop—"Poetry Workshop I"—aimed at teaching introductory students what poetry is *not*. As Villa put it, discussion in this first workshop was designed to demolish pre-conceived ideas in order to lay a foundation for learning what poetry *is*. This book's first fourteen chapters present the material that Villa covered in this workshop.

Villa's second workshop—"Poetry Workshop II"—provided a step-by-step analysis of the specific problems encountered in the composition of a poem. Subjects covered were how a poem begins; the problem of the first line and its propulsion; language and utility of metaphors; versification; lingual and thematic suspensions; valid and invalid details; abstraction in poetry; achieving complexity and intellectual challenge in poetry; direction and unitive flow; balancing of internal and external forms; and poetic

---

1 Lewis Carroll, *Through the Looking Glass*, Chapter 6.

resolution in the last line, bringing the poem to an organic whole. These subjects comprise Chapters 15–25.

Graduates of these first two workshops were then invited to attend "Poetry Workshop III," an advanced seminar conducted at Villa's Greenwich Village apartment in New York City. Supported by Cummings, Villa believed that, after a student had learned the principles of poetry, at least ten years need be devoted to learning language and technique and cultivating his or her life and art before that student could create and write the required language for poetry. Accordingly, Villa taught Workshop III to loyalists—the Editor of this book included—in every year until his death in February 1997, though in 1973 he ceased teaching his other workshops.

Workshop III was not a lecture course. How it was conducted needs recounting to enlighten Villa's process in our awakening to the art of poetry. Typically, this workshop was held on Thursday evenings throughout the year, commencing at 8:00 p.m. Villa would begin with his "table-talk" (a term Villa apparently borrowed from a book edited by J.C. Thornton, *Table Talk by Various Writers from Ben Johnson to Leigh Hunt*,[2] found in Villa's apartment after his death). There, table-talk is described as "at its best... a rare distillation of the wit and wisdom of great men who committed to speech what literary conventions might have forbidden them to write." Villa was a voracious reader and highlighted articles to share with the class. These were not limited to poetic subjects—Villa believed it important that serious poets must lead a good life, quoting W.H. Auden: "God may reduce you on judgment day to tears of shame, reciting by heart the poems you would have written had your life been good."[3] We students labeled this part of Villa's class "Life 101."

Villa also distributed cartoons, many of them from *The New Yorker*, asking us to relate them to poetry. Illustrations in this book will give the reader an idea of this process. Then, if Villa had assigned homework, he asked that it be produced. Homework normally consisted of "Adaptations"—poems students constructed from prose material and occasionally bad verse that Villa had selected as having the potential for successful versification. (The Appendix on Adaptations starts with Villa's instructions as to how to complete these assignments, and a brief discussion of the function of these adaptations is found in Chapters 23 and 25.)

Then, Villa dealt with the poems presented by members of the workshop (unlike his first two workshops in which he discouraged such presen-

---

2 Vol. 906 in *Everyman's Library* (1934)

3 W.H. Auden, "The Cave of Making."

tations). The process of presenting our poems was daunting. Copies were distributed to all present. Villa read the poem. If he did not deem it worthy of discussion, he simply proposed that we move on to the next poem, depositing the unworthy candidate in the wastebasket. If one were lucky, Villa might comment on the poem's failings, but he did not always do so.

A more encouraging response from Villa was: "There may be something to this one; let's see if we can work with it." This signaled that all class members should apply themselves to making something better of this flawed poem. God forbid that anyone just sat there and did not apply himself or herself earnestly to the task. If a student felt that he or she had an improved version and was courageous enough to present it, he or she then went to the blackboard and subjected the revision to the same scrutiny given the initial version. This process was repeated until the class had nothing more to contribute. Villa then promptly presented his revision. In almost all instances, it was superior to anything the class had produced. Discussion of a single poem and the variations frequently continued for hours, making for a long night if, as was usual, several poems were presented.

On rare occasions, a poem was accepted as presented. On even rarer occasions, a student's revision was accepted. This was high tribute, because in either case it was a concession by the Master that even he could not improve it.

Discussions at the third workshop might touch upon any subject—principles taught in Villa's introductory workshops, characteristics of poets or poems that could provide guidance on specific points, how to formulate or recognize a good first line or concluding line, etc. Mainly, however, Workshop III was geared to learning through practice the craft of versification, the subject matter of Chapter 23.

Class continued into the morning—it was not unusual to still be there at 1:00 or 2:00 a.m., sometimes later. The class was "civilized" by the availability throughout the evening of gin martinis (the only drink permitted), adding to the fortitude required to get to the "day job" later the same morning in a condition to function.

Two photographs, taken at Villa's Greenwich Village apartment, show, respectively: 1) where Villa conducted his third workshop and 2) Villa and the Editor at a workshop. The third photograph portrays Villa and workshop members at a 1980 celebration of the publication of the first issue of *BRAVO—The Poet's Magazine,* edited by Villa from 1980 to 1982. John E. Cowen, Villa's Literary Trustee and co-publisher (with the Editor) of *BRAVO*, is holding the magazine in the third photograph.

Villa in his Greenwich Village apartment.

Until his death, Villa continued to develop and hone his theory of poetry. More than 10,000 handwritten notes related thereto are collected at the Houghton Library of Harvard University—notes that Villa intended to add to his voluminous work. Housed there are 13 binders he used in his lectures. These binders, Villa's supplementary notes, and notes taken by students at his lectures are the primary sources for my distillation of his theory of poetry. Villa left no manuscript, finished or unfinished, relating to his theory—merely the binders and notes described above.

While this book goes into detail on poetry and how it is written, the essence of Villa's teachings is found on the back cover of *BRAVO*, where he wrote:

Villa, at a workshop with the Editor.

*BRAVO* Believes That:

- Poetry must have formal excellence
- Poetry must be lyrical
- Poetry is not prose

BEANS ARE OUT…
DIAMONDS ARE IN.

An acquaintance of Villa, W.H. Auden, wrote in 1972: "I can't understand— strictly from a hedonistic point of view—how one can enjoy writing with no form at all. If one plays a game one needs rules, otherwise there is no fun. The wildest poem has to have a firm basis in common sense, and this, I think, is the advantage of formal verse. Aside from the obvious corrective advantages, formal verse frees one from the fetters of

Villa and workshop members at a 1980 celebration of the publication of the first issue of *BRAVO–The Poet's Magazine*.

one's ego."[4] Robert Frost put the matter more succinctly when he observed: "I would as soon write free verse as play tennis without a net."[5]

Villa did not advocate return to the formalism characteristic of earlier poets: strict attention to metrics, adherence to rigid and arbitrary forms, concern with imagery, necessity of rhyming, etc. Rather, Villa presented a theory of modern poetry whereby poems are written organically by refer-

4 W.H. Auden, quoted in *Writers–Photographs by Nancy Compton* (New York: WW Norton, 2005), 28.

5 Robert Frost, Address at Milton Academy, Massachusetts (17 May 1935).

ence to principles, not rules, made to be infringed upon so long as the poet understands, and is faithful to, the overriding principle that a work of art is not what it is *about* but what it *is*: in poetry, its qualities of writing. These make us experience the art.

Villa maintained that the basic and fundamental principles in poetry must be learned, just as fundamental principles in the study of medicine are important to a doctor's education. He stated that "the education of an art object—a poem—begins with the education of the artist himself." If one aspires to be able to write and/or fully appreciate lyric poems, one must grasp the nature and craft of poetry. To the extent these subjects may be taught, they are to be found in this book.

Raised in a prose-conscious environment, we're prone to judge poetry by prose standards and to read poems for their meaning, for what they "say." Many teachers spend an inordinate number of hours with their students trying to fathom what a poet meant to say, judging the poem by prose standards, rather than placing primary focus on the language, the musicality, the versification, the tensions and suspensions of the poetic line and stanza and the poem as a whole, and—first and foremost—its lyricism. What these terms mean in the context of poetry as a fine art, you will learn from reading and understanding this book.

And here is good news. The novice writer and/or reader of poetry needn't have a college degree, be a literature major, pursue a Master of Fine Arts degree, or even attend a poetry workshop to grasp the nature of the poetic process and use the workable tools found herein in crafting and appreciating poetry as a fine art. Villa was a poetic visionary and a Master teacher who set forth his theory in easily-understood terms, making what first seems inaccessible approachable even to the common reader. This is truly a book for anyone.

# EDITOR'S NOTE

There should be no confusion as to my role as Editor. My intention is to present a distillation of José Garcia Villa's theory of poetry just as he presented it at his lectures at City College and the New School and at Poetry Workshop III. I use the term "distillation" because it would be folly for me to claim to present in a book this size all of the relevant information contained in the voluminous Villa materials housed at the Houghton Library. Moreover, I would not want to discourage future scholars from digging deeper—while at the same time assuring the reader that I have attempted to present the *complete* sweep of Villa's theory herein. For my part, I do not believe I left out any important subject matter espoused by Villa, but I leave to future scholars determination of the correctness of that assertion.

As this book is being first published in the Philippines, readers may wonder whether anything is left out with reference or relevance to the Philippines. I cannot recall in all of the lecture materials I reviewed a single specific reference to the Philippines. For one thing, Villa's lecture notes were prepared for presentation to American students at his workshops described above. However, far more important, Villa's theory of poetry is universal, having application to poetry writers anywhere on the planet. Further comment on this subject may be found in the Editor's Epilogue and in blog entries on the Editor's website: www.theoryofpoetry.com—where contemporary applications of Villa's principles are discussed.

Notwithstanding the "distillation" described above, the voice in this book is Villa's voice, without any substantive input of my own other than clarifications, which I have taken great care to insert in footnotes. Villa's "voice" is taken primarily from his lecture materials and, secondarily, from notes taken at his lectures and recollections thereof. Villa intended to use these materials as a foundation for his own book, but energy and health failed him. In his literary papers sorted after his death, there was no hint that he ever started a manuscript to convert his lecture notes to book form. Though he did not directly ask me to take up that task for him, he indicated to me and others that he wished his unpublished writings published by his Literary Estate. With the cooperation and assistance of his Literary Trustee, I have happily shouldered that responsibility. My "editing" consisted mainly of providing continuity to Villa's lectures by breaking them into chapters and eliminating repetitions attributable to the lecture format—a cross reference now serves the same purpose as Villa's repetitions. (Many repetitions are still to be found herein, where I believed the repetition to have been deliberate to emphasize the importance of the subject matter, i.e., repetition for effect.) In addition, as Editor, I was selective in choosing from among cartoons, clippings, etc., Villa utilized in his lectures to illustrate poetic principles.

In his lectures, Villa used the pronoun "I" when assuring his students what poetry is and how it is written, and the pronoun "we" when stating what we collectively could expect to learn in his workshops. In general, I have retained these usages, with the understanding that the "I" refers to Villa and that the "we" refers to the readers of this book.

In clarification, while the "I" in this book refers to Villa as the source of the information conveyed herein, as Villa explained in his lectures:

> Although the lyric poet constantly uses the pronoun "I," we cannot accuse him of egotism—the poet's "I" is not necessarily self-referential—the pronoun enlarges and transcends the merely personal—it now becomes a Mythic and Dramatic "I"— what is called a "persona" greater than just the self of the poet writing.[6]

While Villa said this in the context of poetry and not in terms of usage in his lectures—which of course were prose—nevertheless I think it is fair to say that in his lectures Villa was using a spiritual and transpersonal "I." As you will discover, Villa was not just expressing his personal views on poetry. He was synthesizing the views of many fine poets, artists, critics and scholars, male and female, knowledgeable about the poetic process.

Along the same lines, Villa frequently quoted from these sources, demonstrating that he was not making his theory out of whole cloth. By these quotations, Villa was presenting the considered reflections and conclusions of many persons highly knowledgeable about art and the art of poetry specifically. He used these quotations both to flesh out his own judgments and to demonstrate wide agreement on the principles of fine art and poetry he advocated.

Villa, sometimes but not uniformly, gave specific attribution to the source of these quotations. Frequently, however, he did not. I considered tracking down the source documents to insure the faithfulness of the quotation to the original text and to ascertain whether the punctuation and

---

6 See Chapter Twelve, p. 54

emphasis came from the source or from Villa's elaboration. However, not wishing to interrupt the flow with such details of original attribution, I chose not do so. The reader should treat these quotations in the same spirit, and not assume that each quotation is 100% accurate or even that the person to whom the quotation is attributed would agree with the use to which Villa put it.

Villa advised that, though his theory of poetry was far more comprehensive than could be found elsewhere, much could be learned by consulting other sources of learning on the subject, principally Paul Valéry's *The Art of Poetry.*[7]

---

7 Paul Valéry, *The Art of Poetry*, Bollingen Series XLV 7 (Princeton: Princeton University Press, 1958).

# Poetry is

## CHAPTER ONE

# In Poetry, What You Don't Know Can Hurt You

This book teaches a theory of poetry—a poetics—or a grammar of poetry, using "grammar" in an enlarged sense: not in the sense of prescriptive rules but as a constitutional system of poetry. "The imperative of poetry," said Paul Valéry, "is a poetics."

My [Villa's] experience with poetry workshops taught by others is that there exists no background of shared knowledge so that people can converse with and understand one another. There is no consensus of definition, no common frame of reference, no shared resources, only divisions of interpretation.

This is a book on the clarification of what poetry is and what poetry does—of what poetry is not and what poetry does not do.

Within, we will try to give poetry definition instead of leaving it vague—we will try to give it more precision of identification. We will learn to judge it by trained standards.

If you want to write poetry, you should know what poetry is. This is a simple proposition, but highly controversial in these times of self expression, confessional poetry and free verse.[8]

In this book, the reader will learn poetry as the art of serious writing in verse and not poetry as a mere pastime. We will investigate poetry as a precise literary art, in terms of the art of letters, in terms of its own medium—that of the art of language.

We will learn the specifics of poetry: its special qualities and characteristics, its special structural necessities. We will bring clarity, order and intelligence to the concept of poetry.

There are three subjects, however, that we will not study in this book: 1) metrics, 2) arbitrary or fixed forms, and 3) imagery. Your minds will be cleansed and freed from these three subjects.

---

8 As to how the term "free verse" is used in this context, see Chapter 11.

What is called metrics (iambic, trochaic, dactyl, anapest, spondee, etc.) are merely the popular mechanics of verse. No good poet sits down to write a poem and says to himself or herself: "I'm going to write this poem in iambic pentameter." The poet only finds what his or her meter is after he or she has written the poem.

I can assure you that no good poet ever literally scanned his or her lines—he or she has an inner ear that tells him or her that the lines are moving either rightly or wrongly.

Another subject not covered in this book is arbitrary or fixed forms, such as the sonnet, triolet, villanelle, sestina, etc. To construct a poem to a mold is arbitrary. Poetry is not about fixed forms, but about form. Form (in the singular) is organic form; a poem should grow of itself; it should have a natural, organic growth, by its own pattern and measurements.

Dylan Thomas said: "Poetry finds its own form; form should never be superimposed; the structure should rise out of the words." This is because the poet is controlling the words.

The third subject we will not study—imagery—relates to things that have very little to do with the poetic process. Whatever images are in a poem were brought to it by the choice of language. The poet needs words and music, not images. He needs good-sounding words because he must make music. Images do not make music.

However, the word that you choose for its sound and rhythm will pop up an image. The choice of another word will pop up a different image.

Also, you may be surprised to learn that there can be good poems without any images at all.

• • •

In poetry, what you don't know can hurt you. It is better to know than not to know.

To love poetry is to study it. This of course will give you the right premises, the right basis, the right reasons for writing and reading poetry.

We will not discuss technique until much later in this book.

Your concept of poetry forms the poem's invisible means of support. The education of an art object—a poem—begins with the education of the artist himself.

There are innumerable books about poetry, but they yield only random, though significant, observations on poetry—a facet here, an aspect there, another aspect somewhere else. The best of these books is Paul Valéry's *The Art of Poetry.*

But as for an organized and structured theory of poetry—there is none, until now. This book is the product of notes that I started in 1951 under a grant from the Bollingen Foundation and later from the Rockefeller Foundation, for a theory of poetry.

In the construction of a building, it is necessary to raze the old structure to make way for the new one. So this book begins with a discussion about poetry. The debris, the rubble, the junk that we unearth during this discussion we will discard—until the site is level and clear, and your minds are open to the learning that follows.

Poetry is, first of all, *language, music* and *form.* Content or meaning is *always secondary* —or even unimportant—in poetry. Thomas Hardy said: "If Galileo had said in verse that the world moved, the Inquisition might have left him alone."

Ned Rorem, the composer, said: "Why do I write music? Because I want to hear it—it's simple as that."

As will be developed in detail later, prose is concerned with meaning but, in poetry, a poem should not start with meaning. Meaning has a specialized role in poetry that will be discussed in the context of "Great Poetry." (Chapter 14) For present purposes, the "poet" who begins a poem with the deliberate intention of "saying something" is not working by the poetic process. Consequently, part of the debris that you must clear if you want to write poetry is the notion that poetry can be written by the prose process.

As a result, I would counsel you, if you truly want to write poetry, to fence yourself off from novels and short stories. The less you expose yourself to fiction, the better it is for your poetry. You must be single-minded and serve only one master. The discipline of poetry—as you will find from reading this book—is the exact reverse of that of prose. Fiction is pernicious and harmful to poetry. The giving up of fiction is one of the occupational demands of poetry. You may read expository or informational prose, such as history, biography, criticism and philosophy, but if you are truly serious about writing poems you must specialize in poetry because poetry has a tightrope esthetic. It is, in Wallace Stevens' words, "a Scholar's Art."

One should be willing to accept limits—to know one field well is enough. Stevens said: "I like to think in a corner."

The writing of poetry requires one's whole being, the thorough integration of all faculties concurrently at work. Poetry is not easy; it is difficult work.

An untrained reader of poetry does not want to have a critical attitude—all he wants is a simple pleasure-or-pain reaction to what he reads.

He does not understand poetry or even want to understand poetry so much as to have poetical feelings.

W.H. Auden was once asked: "What must I do to understand the poems of E. E. Cummings and Dylan Thomas?" He answered: "Be born again."

Robert Frost, when asked by someone the meaning of one of his poems, replied: "You want me to say it over again in other and worse English?"

The poet, Laura Riding, observed:

> The chief condition the ordinary reader makes about poetry is that *it shall not be difficult.* For if it is difficult he must *think in unaccustomed ways,* and thinking to the plain reader, beyond the range necessary for practical purposes of living, is unsettling and dangerous.

But you cannot read a poem with your mind alone or your heart alone—actually you must read it first with your ears and your eyes. This is because the value of poetry is not so much in its subject matter as in the sensory qualities of the poem.

Sir Herbert Read said:

> The cadences of poetry are just as sensational as the tones of music. Many people will readily admit to being tone deaf in music. I have met very few people who admit to being tone deaf in poetry.

If you do not hear the music of poetry and if you do not see the physicality of a poem, you are not meant for poetry at all. Poetry is not so much a thinking object as it is a sensory and sensuous object.

Since prose is written to communicate idea or meaning, if you do not study the art of poetry, you will believe that poetry also is written to communicate meaning. The "poems" of prose-writers have a laxness and imprecision of language—they are not language yet for they use the language of prose. That satisfies prose; it does not satisfy poetry. And these prose "poems" have a looseness of technique—prose-writers do not know how to tighten the vise of a poem to that finality of authority that is required.

An understanding of the differences between prose and poetry, which will be discussed in great detail below, is perhaps the most important aspect of the demolition of your pre-conceived ideas that you must accomplish in order to lay the foundation to become a poet.

When you come to poetry, you must come to it initially by temperament—by gut involvement—because you have a visceral affinity with it. It appeals to you and moves you and you are then an instinctual poet. This is where poetry for you becomes a "sacred calling." And, secondly, you must be called to poetry by principle—with awareness that there are things about poetry that must be studied and learned. And, unless you have this "technical call," you cannot be a poet.

To learn to write poetry, you must first learn to read poetry. You must learn to be a connoisseur of poetry—and to be a connoisseur you must be a constant reader of poetry, not just a casual reader. You must read to discover your poetic inheritance and to lean upon and be guided by its achievements before you attempt what you might think are new explorations.

You must in addition read the modern poets, for we must be in equilibrium with and at pace with our own time. As the philosopher Heraclitus said centuries ago: "You cannot step twice into the same river, for other waters are continually flowing in."[9]

Since you aspire to be poets, you are not to read the poems in the way the ordinary reader does. The ordinary reader reads only the subject matter, not the writing. Most readers are quick to feel the sentiments but slow to read the writing. The same subject matter can be packaged in good or bad writing. The same piece of music can be played well or badly. The same play can be staged well or badly. The same piece of fabric can be made into an elegant dress or a sloppy dress. Just as there is a cut and style to dressmaking, so there is a cut and style to writing poetry. Read the cut and style of the writing first, not the subject matter of the poem.

Reading the writing means reading the technical excellences, searching for the "writerly" aspect of the writing—with awareness of what is going on in the *medium itself* (which in poetry is language). It means scrutinizing and observing what is happening in the *language* and in the *form*: the activity of words *as words* (rather than as meaning)—how the words are chosen and juxtaposed, how the sounds flow and blend together, how the lines move from one to the next, and from one stanza to another—how the

---

9 Villa's poetry workshops utilized two anthologies of poetry as reading material for the class to study the good poets: Conrad Aiken, ed., *Twentieth Century American Poetry* (New York: Modern Library edition, Random House, 1963) and Oscar Williams, ed., *A Pocket Book of Modern Verse* (New York:Washington Square Press, Simon & Schuster, 1958). Both are out of print but still obtainable via internet booksellers, among others. Recommended by Villa as the very best in modern poets to be found in these anthologies—the poets against whom would-be poets should measure their work—are, in alphabetical order: George Barker, E. E. Cummings, Emily Dickinson, Richard Eberhart, Robert Frost, Gerard Manley Hopkins, Wilfred Owen, John Crowe Ransom, Edith Sitwell, Wallace Stevens, and Dylan Thomas.

poem is finally closed. These are the technical and "writerly" qualities of being a poet.

In other words, you must learn to read technically, watching out for the delights that technical virtuosity affords—because the art is in the writing. Form and content are divisible—in good works they are divided; they are not divided in bad works. The form is the created work; the content is only raw material.

A work of art is not what it is about, but what it actually is: its qualities of writing. These are what make us experience the art. If the work only impresses you emotionally and mentally, it is nothing unless it impresses you aesthetically first. To be a poet, one needs technical qualifications, rather than mental or emotional qualifications.

After reading a poem, the question to ask is: "How did the poet do it?" —not: "What did he say?"

In art, you must look for the aesthetic experience, not the emotional or semantic one. Your status as a poet does not depend on how you feel toward life, or on how good your ideas are, or on how well-meaning you are, *but on how well you write.*

The reader can be moved by subject matter, for example, an account of the last American killed in Vietnam after the signing of the peace agreement. This incident and our being moved by it are, however, not art—in order for this raw material to become art, something must be done. Satisfying artistic form must be provided by an artist.

For many readers, their experience in poetry has not been an experience of poetry so much as an experience of content—for them, the message always looms larger than the medium.

Experience is without words—it is made of feeling and not of language. But from these feelings-experiences, we can create another feeling-experience that is made of language and that is called literature. Literature is made of expert language that yields a feeling-experience.

In other words, art is the reality of life transformed into the condition and reality of art. The inspiration for art is art itself—and not nature or life experiences. You can become poets only by paying attention to the conditions of poetry: by paying attention to the delights that the technical virtuosity of the writing affords, to the quality and movements and resonances of its language, to the patterns of language evolved and to the structural form achieved by the poem. When you can achieve positive, technical effects, then you can be called a poet.

In Greek, the word for art is "*tekhne*"—and that means technique, referring to the manner of execution. Paul Valéry wrote: "The execution of the poem is the poem." That means when you have good execution you have a good poem. Being poetic in content does not make the poem good poetry. Bad poetry may also be poetic in content. And even good prose may be poetic in content.

This is why a poem can never be evaluated merely by having it read to an audience. A poem must be seen with the eyes if one is to judge it at all as a poem, because versification and form can be judged only with the aid of the eyes. Form in poetry cannot be heard, not even if you have a hundred ears, only seen.

At the beginning of one's studies of poetry, *theory* is more important and more practical than practicing writing poems. Without a base of knowledge as to how poetry is written, writing and presenting poems at poetry workshops or for publication is not a good use of your time.[10]

10 Villa discouraged his students from presenting poems in his first workshop, but did not preclude them from doing so. In the event that they wanted to present their efforts to the class, Villa advised them to keep them to a maximum of 15 lines, explaining that: "If you are going to be good poets, you should learn the economy of poetry. Brevity is the economics of beauty. The tendency and nature of poetry is to contract, to condense and pull inward—rather than expand. Its intensity demands this contraction—for intensity is difficult to sustain. Diffuseness is not a virtue but a fault in poetry. Great poems have been written within these limits."

## CHAPTER TWO

# Poetry is Not Self Expression

Much of what passes as "poetry" these days is self expression, which is nothing but romantic infantilism and baby talk. Art may express emotion, but it is emotion that springs from the work of art itself. It is generated emotion, generated by the work as it grows. It is emotion that is not generated from the condition of the author.

In the medium of language, there are two kinds of expression: 1) basic expression, and 2) creative expression. Basic expression is for communication purposes, and it can be oral or written. The important thing is the direct communication of what is to be said or written, as in newscasts, in business letters, in books of information, and in lectures.

Creative expression manifests itself in the fields of poetry and creative prose (poetry is always creative; prose is not). The important thing is artistry: the grace of expression and shapeliness of form. Creative expression does not communicate meaning in the sense of a flat, direct statement; rather it works by nuances, by indirection. Its method is sensory.

The good poet distances himself from his or her work—he or she views it objectively. Instead of having an ego function, art is ego-bending—it curbs the ego. An artist is not self-serious but art-serving—that is the impersonal principle of art. The last thing to matter to art is the artist's personal self.[11]

As Paul Valéry put it, what you have in self expression is "the libretto of the nervous system."

What is necessary in art is not self expression, but self constraint and impersonalization. It makes for more durable art. And yet, although art is impersonal, it is never depersonalized. It will bear the stamp of the author's personality.

You must go to poetry not to fulfill emotional needs but to fulfill aesthetic needs. Even if a poem springs from feeling, this feeling should be objectified into an art object, for a poem first of all is an art object. An art

---

11 This is what W.H. Auden alluded to when, in the quotation in the Introduction to this book, he wrote that: "Aside from the obvious corrective advantages, formal verse frees one from the fetters of one's ego."

object can be achieved only by paying attention to the medium and to form, not to the ego. Engagement with the medium and form in poetry means acquiring a sense of language and technical control.

Good writing doesn't just happen. Self expression always just happens. It is pre-rational in the sense of being done without thinking. Writing is thinking in terms of the medium.

The good poet maintains a superb indifference to subject matter, because he or she is writing the poem without knowing the subject matter—he or she is to discover the subject matter and emotion only after the poem is finished.

To be a poet means that one first has to solve the linguistic problem. By "linguistic," I don't mean having an extensive knowledge of the meaning of words or having a large vocabulary, but the tackling of language to have a way with words. The poet structures words so that they become more than words and become an artistic structure.

T.S. Eliot wrote: "The more perfect the artist, the more completely separate in him will be the man who suffers and the mind which creates." Instead of self expression, let's believe in self suppression. A book review was headed: "Don't Sing Your Crap!" That is good advice. Keep a diary instead, preferably the kind with a lock and key, so that nothing can leak out.

Françoise Gilot, in writing of her life with Picasso, tells of a painting, a still life by Matisse, in Picasso's studio, and observes that: "Each time I saw it I had this feeling of harmony, of vitality, of joy." She once said to Matisse that he must have been very happy when he painted it. He responded: "Ah, that one. Yes, I painted that in Algiers at a time when I was close to committing suicide." There you see the non-relationship between emotion and art.

The meaning of the word "express" is to press out, to tease out—from the words their fullest values—to squeeze out from the language, which is our medium, its best values. The poet presses on language, not the ego.

You must not color your poem with your own psychological problems. See, in particular, Chapter 17 below.

## CHAPTER THREE

# What is Poetry?

To learn poetry, one (who is inexperienced) cannot go immediately to the best poems written—because you are still unaware of the principles that justify them.

Before I can teach you how to write poetry, I must teach you how to think about poetry. Each field of art has its own specialties, its own character, and each art is actually doing something other than other arts are doing—and other than other arts are not doing. Therefore, the study of poetry involves a different angle of perception from a study of the other arts. Each individual art involves a particular imagination that has different demands.

A painter, looking at an object, would observe its pattern, design and colors. A sculptor, looking at the same object, would not notice the colors at all, for he would be looking at the shape, its mass and movement. So if you are interested in colors, you should be a painter.

Although there is a unity among the arts, there is also a great separation among them. The divisions of art are indeed divisions; we are altered in approach by the technological medium we use. Failure to relate your poems to poetic reason can result in failure.

We are so surrounded, conditioned and habituated by prose that we expect all literature to have the properties of prose. We must re-think and reconfigure (decolonize) our minds to poetry and away from prose.

With prose so environmental, we now see why most people are prose-happy and prose-minded—but there are always a few who get prose-unhappiness and these few are the ones who become poets.

When you move from a prose culture to a poetic culture, there is inevitably a culture shock—the difficulty in believing that this new world is utterly so different from the other. A work written with prose intelligence may have no poetic intelligence—what has been good for prose has not been good for poetry. There has been a change of jurisdiction—you are now in a different country or territory.

The method of attack changes, because poetry is a different enterprise entirely. Until we erase the subliminal directives of prose, we shall find it difficult to write or even understand poetry.

We are now going to make a systematic study of poetry—in an order and sequence that grows toward a structure of knowledge and in terms that focus clearly so that poetry no longer is the victim of *mistaken identity*. We will get rid of the notion of do-it-yourself poetics, and instead we will study responsible poetics. We are going to learn the basic design of poetry.

What does "poetry" mean? To the uneducated public, poetry is an umbrella word—it can shelter anything you throw in it or under it. Like "love," poetry is endlessly receptive to quixotic, personal interpretations. Literature is another umbrella word—travel agencies hand out "literature," so do insurance companies, automobile companies, investment banks, the Army, etc. However, to a literature student, the word means *only* the *art* of literature.

Till now, the word "poetry" has been imprecise and catches all varieties of meaning—but it should have one very definite and specific meaning. We must think of poetry as a serious art, not as a popular art. To define is to set boundaries or limits. *Poetry as art is lyrical poetry.*

We must not think of poetry as in the service of something else. We speak loosely of poetry as narrative poetry, satirical poetry, didactic poetry, dramatic poetry, but none of these is related to the *art of poetry*. Narrative poetry, such as the writings of Homer, Dante, Virgil and Chaucer, is poetry in service of telling a story, which today is done better by writing a novel. Dramatic poetry, such as Shakespeare's plays, tells of events that have occurred in the past as though they were occurring in the present. Narrative and dramatic poetry are malpractice of poetry—the story assumes the greatest importance at the expense of the lyrical spirit. They involve verse applied to the matter and uses of prose. Poetry is the frosting on the cake but only in the sense that it is an accompaniment, like music played as an accompaniment to a movie. People who today look for story lines or for ideas in poetry have no poetic intelligence. Except in his sonnets, Shakespeare was not really a poet.

The true meaning of poetry is lyric poetry. Lyric poetry does not have a story or prose function—it has a song function. The poet is a minstrel who sings. Poetry must be lyrical. If you really like poetry, you will hear the sounds of the words as you read them in the way that a musician hears the sounds of the notes on the music sheet.

We are now about to embark on the study of a *theory of poetry*, the aesthetics or science of poetry, an analytic conception of what poetry is, a technical as well as psychological study of poetry. The term "technical" refers to the mechanics of poetry—its external physical side; "psychological" refers to the internal happenings in poetry.

Awareness of the principles of poetry makes the concept of what poetry is and what it is not more intelligible, more meaningful. Poetry is not a general knowledge but a specialist knowledge.

Can poetry be taught? If you know poetry theoretically but not practically (in the writing) you don't know its whole practice. The more complete a practical knowledge of poetry grows, the less it is distinguishable from knowledge of its theory. The theoretical and the practical should fuse and become one. We are going to study a theory of poetry that is full of practical facts. We are also going to study the practice of poetry that is full of theoretical facts. We are going to strive to write poems in accordance with the true nature and character of poetry.

Poetry writing cannot be taught but one can be taught in the sense of guided in the concept of poetry and the craft of poetry—that much can be taught.

In a true poet, always two poets co-exist: 1) the internal poet, the man of intuition and insight—the element that makes one feel and see like a poet, and 2) the external poet, the technical man who constructs the poem. We can be possessed of poetic feelings but without the technical poet in us we cannot write a poem.

There are no rules for writing poetry. Dylan Thomas said: "You make your own rules." But there are principles behind poetry. A principle is a fundamental truth, which exercises a governing or guiding influence over the field. Principles are guidelines of essential character so that poems are made true to their character, and these principles we will study.

By contrast, rules are laws or regulations that are restrictive—they are prescribed orders or directions to which one must conform. Principles are flexible and non-restrictive. Poetry has more non-rules than rules. And restrictive non-rules are principles.

There are many misconceptions about poetry—among them:

1. Poetry tells a story, or must give a moral lesson.
2. Poetry is nothing but emotion expressed in embellished language.
3. Poetry is dressed-up thought (not talking of actual intelligence but trivial and ordinary thoughts).
4. Poetry is mere rhyming.

5. Poetry is mere regularity of rhythm—if that were so, poets would be persons without an inner ear; the music of poetry is not the beat of a mechanical clock or metronome.

What then is "poetry?" Guillaume Appolinaire wrote: "I know that poetry is necessary—but I don't know what for." The value of poetry is thus made dubious and questionable, as it has no utility, serves no practicable purpose, and cannot be used to earn good money.

Nevertheless, it has importance.

- *First,* it is irreplaceable by prose. It does what prose cannot do. Its "say" is not a statement but consists of presenting an afterglow.
- *Second,* the aesthetic discipline of poetry is also an intellectual and ethical discipline—it sharpens the intellectual and moral senses. Poetry becomes a civilization of the human spirit. W.H. Auden said: "God may reduce you on judgment day to tears of shame, reciting by heart the poems you would have written had your life been good." And Kafka said: "Poetry is a disease. But it purifies, it illuminates."
- *Third,* poetry prevents madness—it prevents mental disturbances.

Poetry as humanity, as a way of life, is not a poetic virtue but pertains to the art of living. In this book, we study poetic values, and not the ulterior or humanistic values of poetry.

Even limiting poetry to lyrical poetry, the term "poetry" still remains a broad term.

Poetry can exist as spirit: where poetry is a spiritual coefficient of human nature. Man's heart has a natural, spontaneous internal power—of insight and imagination.

Poetry as spirit is an inward light—an all-embracing sense of good and rightness. That is why Wallace Stevens said: "Poetry is *not* a literary activity—it is vital activity—a part of life itself."

This poetic spirit, being a spiritual force and energy, is spontaneous and uncontrollable—it breaks out of us in unguarded moments and we say things that are poetic without intending to do so. It is especially noticeable in children's speech, in their remarks that can be perfectly astonishing. Examples: Eric (age 3): "I can't look at the sun long. It makes my eyes all out of breath." Or Jonathan (age 3): "The moon is what the sun leaves behind when it goes down."

Robert Frost wrote: "There is more religion outside the church than in, more love outside marriage than in, more poetry outside the verse than in." The long arm of poetry arches from art into life and from life into art.

Poetry is not just the art of versification. It is a whole world where the poetic spirit enters—in life itself where we see beauty or the grace of things—their proportions, relationships, destinies—whenever a fine sense of values enters our lives and tells us that these are truths.

Poetry as spirit springs involuntarily from the human heart. You don't have to do anything for it. But poetry as art is not automatic or spontaneous—it has to be worked for—into the discipline of form. In order to be art, form is mandatory. Poetry as art is always controlled, conscious and deliberate.

Poetry as spirit is in all the arts—it is the essence of all of the arts. However, in poetry as art, an artist is at the helm and he or she imposes pattern and architecture, i.e., form, on the work.

Poetry as spirit is the beauty of humanism, of the good heart, and which may perform poetry in human action, not necessarily into art. It is the intent of all the arts and appears in all of the arts. Put otherwise, all arts are branches of poetry.

Poetry as art—as form—encompasses all the arts. Language plus form is literature; color plus form is painting; mass plus form is sculpture; sound plus form is music. Even prose may be poetic; however, that which is not in verse form cannot be considered poetry.

You can readily see how the loose meaning of poetry these days derives mainly from the fact that there is a spirit of poetry, which does not have to manifest itself in artistic form at all in order to function. The spirit of poetry releases itself directly into life without the need of an artistic form. However, if it is put in artistic form, it becomes one of the arts, and only one is the art called poetry—this is the art of writing in verse. And verse requires technical versification. If you cannot write in verse, in technically good verse, you are not a poet. The art of writing in verse is poetry "reduced to the essence of its active principle," said Paul Valéry.

A poet is a person who has expressional power in word and verse. It is not enough to have the interior poet (the man or woman of intuition)—it is necessary to have the exterior poet, the man or woman who puts that intuition in the form of verse.

The love of language precedes the learning of form. Love of language is instinctive, but knowledge of versification is acquired. The poet has a natural fascination with the potentialities of words, and he or she has a musical delight in them—likes their sound and feel. He or she is not in love with the meaning of words but with their sensory qualities, with their sounds and textures and flow.

W.H. Auden, in *Poets at Work*, asked:

> Why do you want to write poetry? If the young man answers: 'I have important things to say,' then he is not a poet. If he answers: 'I like hanging around words listening to what they say,' then maybe he is going to be a poet.

Robert Frost said: "Poetry begins in delight—and ends in wisdom."

The test of the poet, then, is his or her power to put things not only in words but in verse, in short, his or her power of language and technique.

A poet must be a master of structure. He or she knows 1) how to begin, 2) how to build on what he or she has begun, and 3) how to end, complete the structure. We will go into these subjects in great detail in subsequent chapters. It is only through craft and form that expression in poetry can be successful. This displays the poet's commitment to poetry as an art form.

Let us consider some definitions of poetry formulated by poets universally recognized as among the good poets.

> WALLACE STEVENS: Above everything else, poetry is words; and...words, above everything else, are in poetry, sounds....Poetry is a revelation in words by means of the sounds.

Robert Frost defined poetry as "that which is lost in translation."

In other words, poetry is a verbal and sound event. A poet is a person singing in words instead of in musical notes.

Definitions of poetry may also be metaphorical, as in

> GEORGE SANTAYANA: As common windows are intended only to admit the light, but painted windows also to dye it, and to be an object of attention in themselves as well as a cause of visibility in other things, so, while the purest prose is a mere vehicle of thought, verse, like stained glass, arrests attention in its own intricacies, [confines it in] its own stories, and it is even at times allowed to darken and puzzle in the hope of casting over us a supernatural spell.

> CHRISTOPHER FRY: Poetry is the language in which man explores his own amazement. It is the language in which he says heaven and earth in one word....It has the virtue of being able to say twice as much as prose in

half the time, and the drawback, if you don't happen to give it your full attention, of seeming to say half as much in twice the time.

> DYLAN THOMAS: Poetry is the rhythmic...movement from an overclothed blindness to a naked vision that depends, in its intensity, on the strength of the labour put into the creation of poetry.

Poetry is, in fact, always a definitional problem, an approximation of what poetry is. Still, there is one simple definition of poetry that may possibly be the best: "Poetry is memorable speech." (W.H. Auden)

A piece of poetry becomes a poem when the poem is fully realized as an organic whole—as a finished structure, a complete entity.

> DYLAN THOMAS: An opening line may be a piece of poetry moving toward a poem.

Poetry is the fabric; the poem is the completed suit. A poem is more than the sum of its parts. Poetry, as a literary art, exists as poems. Poetry is not the art of writing poetry, paradoxical as that may seem, but the art of writing poems.

The poet's insight adds depth and ballast to the poem; it is abstract. The poem, on the other hand, is concrete, a manifestation of the art—factual evidence that the art exists. It is the form that will do for art.

Pierre Reverdy, the French poet, maintained that there is no love, only proofs of love. By the same token, we can say that there is no poetry, only proofs of poetry. And the proofs of poetry are poems.

## CHAPTER FOUR

# Differences Between Poetry and Prose

Poetry and prose are in words. They are verbal acts, employing the same medium of language. But poetry is not prose chopped up in short lines. Commercial advertisements use short lines but are not poetry.

Poetry does not get confused with painting because the latter is not a verbal act; the same is true of the other non-verbal arts.

We must understand the differences between poetry and prose so that we can dis-entwine the two. In doing so, we will be speaking of prose in terms of "normal" (mainstream) prose and not in terms of prose that has poetic effects such as the writings of Virginia Woolf, James Joyce and Thomas Wolfe.

We will compare poetry and prose face to face as well as side by side.

There are artistic truths just as there are scientific truths—scholars, like scientists, do not set out to prove anything but the truth. The scholar alters his or her ideas to agree with the facts. He or she does not create truths—they are already there.

To start with the comparison, there are differences in how prose and poetry look on the page. Poetry is short in size and in the length of lines; prose is long and set out in solid paragraphs.

They differ in their aim and function. The aim and function of poetry is to give pleasure and delight, not through its meaning but through its language.

> DYLAN THOMAS: "I myself do not read poetry for anything but pleasure... All that matters about poetry is the enjoyment of it."

On the other hand, the aim and function of prose is to communicate subject matter, and the language used to communicate is unimportant and forgettable.

Poetry must not only give pleasure, but *immediate* pleasure—if you do not attain delight by the 8th or 10th line, what you are reading is not very good as poetry.

> WILLIAM WORDSWORTH: The poet writes under one restriction only, namely, that of the necessity of giving immediate pleasure.

Poetry cannot afford to go slack like prose. Poetry is an intoxicating cocktail whereas prose is a meat-and-potatoes medium.

Meaning is only an accidental power of poetry. It is accidental because the words the poet uses happen to have meaning.

> PAUL VALÉRY: "Prose flies to its meaning, to its purely mental translations and is lost [as language]...for meaning is its final aim."

In prose, the words function like a projector, projecting onto the screen of the reader's mind the meaning of the prose word. The word has left and is dissolved as no longer necessary to the transmission of the mental concept.

> VALÉRY: The essence of prose is to *perish*...i.e., to be *understood*, which is the same as to say, to be dissolved...entirely replaced by the image or concept.

William Troy, the literary and film reviewer, wrote:

> The reader of prose no longer has any use for this language after it has done its work. Paragraph by paragraph, sentence by sentence, prose gives up the ghost. It's being dissolved into whatever it is about...in which service it is really employed.

Unlike prose, the meaning in poetry comes in only subconsciously; it is never deliberately injected in. Poetry is a voyage of discovery; it starts from scratch; it has a chartless journey. It does not know where it is going—until the last line comes with a sudden enlargement of the world. Prose is planned parenthood; poetry is accidental pregnancy.

In later chapters, when the principles of poetry have been defined more clearly than they have been at this point, we will amplify on the differences between prose and poetry.

**CHAPTER FIVE**

# Magic and Genesis in Poetry

## MAGIC IN POETRY

Aladdin's lamp was magical because it could produce instant results. The genie appeared instantly when the lamp was rubbed. This is certainly true of poetry, for good poetry produces immediate delight. Magic is something marvelous and extraordinary that casts a mysterious spell on us. Magic gives poetry a narcotic or hypnotic effect.

One reacts to poetry instantly and viscerally, without the need for complete understanding. Magic has more to do with the medium than the content. Good poetry is incantatory through language itself.

By contrast, the language of prose has no wildness or mystery to it—you can catch what it says, but the language of good poetry has something elusive and wild about it. Robert Frost: "Poetry is like a wild-game preserve. It's where wild things live. This is the ultimate in poetry, and it has to be there."

With the magician—although we clearly know that he will produce a rabbit or saw a woman in half—what entrances us is not the rabbit or the woman but how he does it. We are surprised by the mystery of the medium.

Poetry surprises by the medium, which is language.

When the language of prose becomes magical (as, say, with Thomas Wolfe, Hortense Calisher and Virginia Woolf), it begins to assume qualities that are not in its proper field. It is abnormal prose.

When we say that such prose is "poetic," we are saying the magic of poetry resides mainly in its language and its music—and that is what poetic prose tries to do. But it is trespassing.

On the other hand, when poetry is lacking in magic, we say such verse is "prosaic" or "prosy" (prosaic in the sense of unexciting in subject matter; prosy in the sense of unexciting in language). Thus the subject is prosaic but the style is prosy. Many contemporary poems are both prosaic and prosy at the same time.

## GENESIS IN POETRY

Now we are turning to a subject which, if you do not learn it, you will always be writing the wrong poems. It is a subject you may find difficult to believe.

In the movie *Gentlemen's Agreement*, a journalist (played by Gregory Peck) is asked: "Do you get your ideas first and then write, or do you write first and then get your ideas?" Peck's response: "I don't understand your question."

Why? Because a journalist is a prose writer, and knows only one way of writing: getting the ideas first and then writing them down. He cannot conceive of any other way of writing.

"Genesis" is the method of origination, the way something is formed, the method of creation. Here, we are inquiring how you begin your poems.

Behind the writing of a poem is the aesthetic impulse, the desire to create with language a disinterested work of art. It is disinterested because it has no desire to communicate a message but simply an artistic structure.

Many people start their "poems" from meaning. Meaning is the graveyard of poetry. If you have a thought for a poem, you must dismiss it immediately.

Since poems, like stories and essays, generally have meaning, people tend to mistake this effect as the cause—people who write poetry without studying what it is work the wrong way around.

Thus the prose process and the poetic process are two different creative processes. They revolve around one thing only: presence or absence of subject matter or idea at the start.

Prose has meaning before the writing begins, a pre-calculated plan. Katherine Anne Porter: "Every story begins with an ending." She said: "When I begin a story...I must know a story by heart and I must write [as if] from memory."

Margaret Mitchell wrote her last chapter first. It gave her, she said, something to push toward.

> ANTON CHEKHOV, the Russian master of the short story, proclaimed: [I]f an artist boasted to me of having written a story without a previously settled design, I should call him a lunatic.

> A.J. CRONIN: A good novel should be written in your head before you put pen to paper.

In prose, the idea exists before the actual writing begins. This is true whether the prose is a novel, short story, play, history or philosophy. In prose, the important thing is not to start the work until you have command of the idea.

However, the genesis of poetry is, as Paul Valéry put it, "the very lack and black that create." In a way, the spirit of poetry is related to the spirit of Zen—that emptiness that enlightens.

The poet Stephen Spender wrote:

> I am conscious of a stream of words, which seem to pass through my mind, without their having a meaning, but they have a sound, a sound of passion, or a sound recalling poetry that I know. Again, sometimes when I am writing, the music of the words I am trying to shape takes me far beyond the words, I am aware of a rhythm, a dance, a fury, which is as yet empty of words.

Writing poems is a thinking-out process where the poet is still trying to find his or her meaning in the course of making the poem. The poem assumes a semantic sense only as the poem grows and develops.

> T.S. ELIOT: I wonder what an 'intention' means! One doesn't know quite what it is that one wants to get off the chest until one's got it off. But, I couldn't apply the word 'intention' to any of my poems ... the idea simply comes.

Robert Frost's oft-quoted observation that the poem "begins in delight and ends in wisdom" comes with this explanation: "It begins in delight, it inclines to the impulse, it assumes direction with the first line laid down, it runs a course of lucky events, and ends in a clarification of life."

A poem must be a revelation, or a series of revelations, as much for the poet as for the reader.

Archibald MacLeish, in a blurb for his book *The Human Season: Selected Poems, 1926–1972*, was quoted as saying:

> What this book says I never said before. It's not my story, it's the poems: what they think they know when they put themselves together.

The poetic process starts from the energy and self-kindling of language itself. When you begin a poem with a meaning in mind, that meaning—instead of building the poem up—undermines and pulls it down. A poem that starts with meaning has a birth defect.

> W.H. AUDEN: In poetry you have a form—looking for a subject.

A prospective poet would do well to think about a sign in an optometrist's office: "If you don't see what you want, you're in the right place."[12]

In poetry, the idea is the outcome, the consequence. The poet is aware of language and its sensory quality of music first—he writes from that to the interior of an idea. The poem will make its own meaning from language, not from the poet.

In this, poetry is very close to music. Ned Rorem said: "Composers... don't tell the music where to go—it leads them." David Amrau: "Writing music is like building a bridge. You don't know if you'll reach the other side."

> W.H. AUDEN: The bystander thinks that the poet has something to say, *therefore* he wrote this poem. The poet *knows better*. He wrote because he had to write and subsequently it became evident to him, to his great *amazement*, that he had something to say.

> CHRISTOPHER MORLEY: Poetry is the perfect expression of something you *didn't know you wanted to say*.

It is the language and the music that are doing the thinking. Poetry is creation as revelation.

> RICHARD EBERHART: Poetry is an evocation, a crystallization from the cloud of unknowing... The poet defines himself *as he goes along*.

Each poem is a revelation—of the poet's mind and of his or her spirit—which he or she did not know consciously before. E.M. Forster, in a lecture he gave at Harvard in 1947, best described the creative state of poetry as follows:

> What about the creative state? In it, a man is taken out of himself. He lets down, as it were, a bucket into the unconscious and draws up something which is normally beyond his reach. He mixes this thing with his normal experience and out of the mixture he makes a work of art.

Cummings described the finished poem as "always the beautiful answer who asks a more beautiful question."

---

12 Villa reported that he asked his friend and mentor, Cummings: "Is my way of writing poetry odd because when I started a poem I started from nothing?" Cummings responded: "Who does?" Villa received the same response from Mark Van Doren, Conrad Aiken, Richard Eberhart, Edith Sitwell, and Archibald MacLeish.

HONORÉ DE BALZAC: A man does not recognize as his own what he has written *as a poet*.

Another poet, Jean Burden, wrote:

The poet is making a self as well as a poem….No poet comes out of a poem the same person he was when he went in.

In effect, the poem becomes the poet's way of experiencing life. That experience in the poem occurred only because of the writing of the poem—only in the process of writing. It was not an experience at all before the poem was made.

A poem may say anything—or it may say nothing at all, as in pure poetry, which we will study in Chapter 13.[13]

---

13 Villa wrote a poem, often appearing in anthologies, which describes magic in poetry. He said this poem was written in a dream and, when he awakened, the poem wrote itself and he was merely the scribe, making no further revisions. That poem is:

First, a poem must be magical,
Then musical as a sea-gull.
It must be a brightness moving
And hold secret a bird's flowering.
It must be slender as a bell,
And it must hold fire as well.
It must have the wisdom of bows
And it must kneel like a rose.
It must be able to hear
The luminance of dove and deer.
It must be able to hide
What it seeks, like a bride.
And over all I would like to hover
God, smiling from the poem's cover.

## CHAPTER SIX
# The Kinetics of Poetry

The word "kinetics" is from the Greek word "*kinesis*," which means dynamics—the play of forces at work—which causes movement.

The activism of language propels both the structure and the meaning of the poem.

Edgar Degas, the painter, tried to write verses and considered them failures. He complained to his friend, the poet Stéphane Mallarmé: "Yours is a hellish craft. I can't manage to say what I want and yet I am full of ideas...."

"My dear Degas," Mallarmé answered, "one does not make poetry with ideas, but with *words*."[14] We can say further that poetry is made *by* words.

In poetry, the language is self-kindling—it generates further language. Each succeeding line is provoked into being by the preceding line and language. Each word and phrase directly affects the choice and qualities of the following words. Poetry is an ongoing discovery process. When language directs your poem, there is a chance the result may be poetry.

The poetic process needs only words and the sensory and musical qualities of those words. Yet those words by themselves can propel toward structure and meaning.

The poet, through his or her love of words for their own sake, for their sounds and textures especially, is able to explore his or her subconscious, the contents of which become revealed as surprises. The poem as it proceeds is wired for anything. It scouts around for meaning and may or may not pick up anything. Poetry's choice is to make choices, but it makes these choices by sound and textures.

Meaning arrives impromptu, subconsciously, and tangentially, through the forces and activity of language. Unexpected meanings are the norm in poetry as a result.

That which was unconscious in the text (because the text was moving mainly by sounds and textures), when it gathers itself up at the end of the poem, becomes the meaning of the poem.

---

14 This is as described by Valèry in *The Art of Poetry*, 63.

The communicative function of language—which is to mean—cannot be expunged. So a poem picks up individual meanings. They accrete and the poem picks up more and more thought as it goes along. By the end of the poem, the poet has evolved and achieved a body of thought—a content of idea through the accumulative use of words. The accumulation creates meanings as a byproduct—but only as a byproduct—because the poet was primarily using these words as sounds and textures.

> MARY MCCARTHY: You must listen to the language; that language tells you what you want to say. If some word is sticking out of a sentence [line], say, and it looks ugly, it is telling you what you don't want to say. Language is continually giving you messages.

> ROBERT FROST: A poem is never a put-up job....It *finds* its thought and succeeds—or doesn't find it and comes to nothing.... A poem, particularly, must not begin thought-first.... Its meaning is something you didn't know you know.

In poetry, you don't try to say nothing and you don't try to say something—but you do say something. Poetry chooses to be nothing except what it may possibly become.

In poetry, there is a simultaneous double creation: While the creation of language is happening, the creation of meaning is also happening. Language and meaning arrive concomitantly, concurrently as a single event. The poet's language not only creates its meaning but also the subsequent language.

Poetry is both creator and expressor. Poetry creates idea, thus creator. Poetry expresses the idea, thus expressor. The language of prose is not a creator at all—it is an expressor only.

What is said in prose is only a playback. As James Agee put it, prose is a "mere re-digestion of a pre-digestion." It is a mere replication of a finished mental blueprint.

Strictly speaking, the poetic process is the creative process. The prose process is only creative in its first phase, which happens in the mind. It has finished its creative process when the writing begins. In the poetic process, the creative process is in the writing itself, in the medium itself.

CHAPTER SEVEN

# Language

The medium of language is the instrument on which the poet is playing. Poetry is the miracle of the imagination shining on language.

Elizabeth Bowen, the distinguished English novelist, wrote: "Plot must further the novel toward its object. What object? The non-poetic statement of a poetic truth." The "poetic truth" in prose and in the other arts is still poetry as spirit. The poetic truth here exists only as a kernel, not as a physical artistic body of work. The centric view of poetry is poetic truth within the body of poetry—which means poetic truth in the form of verse. Poetry is the poetic statement of a poetic truth.

Thus, although the heart of both prose and poetry is poetic truth, the essential difference between prose and poetry lies not only in their major differences in genesis and kinetics but in the major difference in their language. Poetry creates a space in which language celebrates itself.

With notable exceptions, practically every line I read in today's poetry is a mishap in language as well as a mishap in craft. It reminds me of what *Time Magazine* described as "unmemorable flatted verse…, an unnecessary and misguided burden upon the ear and the imagination."

In terms of cause and effect, prose chooses language to suit its meaning, whereas poetry chooses meaning to suit its words.

In poetry, language develops from itself—there is no thought to direct the choice of words. Poetry bends meaning to serve the purpose of language, which is to have the right music and texture. Only the sensory and musical qualities of words will direct movement and growth.

Words in poetry are there, first, as verbal objects. They are there not only as signs—they are a verbal reality, a luminous presence. Important in poetry are the physical and sensory values of the words in their formal relations with one another.

The poet quarrels with the ordinary language of prose. It is too *un*sensual and commonplace. Dylan Thomas said: "The diction of prose is not even tailor-made but ready-to-wear." So the poet dramatizes language and heightens it by the deliberate use of sounds and textures, invests it with verbal values.

The poet's language is of his or her own devising—it is very personal. This is because it is crafted piece by piece—word by word—phrase by phrase. This is verbal technique, where the language is structured in close-up terms, musically and texturally.

Prose only has a technique of total structure, which poetry also has. Poetry has a double craft, where prose only has a single craft. The language of poetry becomes a mode of action, rather than simply a means of communication. It is a transmitter of energy because it is charged language. The language of prose is static verbally but poetry acts out the experience that it contains. The language of poetry makes enactments of the meanings it conveys.

Goethe explained that he did not write from his experience, for instance his love affairs, but that he tended—unconsciously—to experience what he would come to write. The language of poetry is able to provide us with a direct experience—the words are like actors actualizing experience before our eyes. Only that particular language of the poem could have released that particular feeling.

In reading poetry, the mind is active because of the challenges of language. In reading prose, the mind is passive (like watching a movie). Prose is for the exploration of ideas—and this is its greatest role and function. In this role, prose is valid and as great as poetry.

In considering the role of language in poetry, we must deal with the question: "Is language a system of meanings?" If the answer is yes, then we must consider whether, in emphasizing sounds over meanings, poetry is then untrue to the nature of language—for the poet (as I have explained) must create delight by the language itself without depending on meaning. In poetry, we are dealing with the physicality of language, with its special energies as the art of speech. We are dealing with language primarily as sound values, as a system of sounds whose purpose is to generate delight.

Language is *not*, however, a system of meanings—it *is* a system of sounds. Thus, the same sounds have different meanings in the various languages. For example, "ciao" in Italian means "Hi" or "So long"; "chow" in English means food; and "chow" in Chinese means any of a breed of medium-sized dogs having certain bodily characteristics. The sound is meaningless in the sense it can convey different meanings. The language is not the meaning; the language is the sounds only.

When emptied of meaning, language is a system of sounds; that is all. Each language has different sounds for the same meaning. For example, in English we say: "You are very beautiful"; in Spanish: "Eres muy linda"; and in German: "Du bist sehr schön."

Superimposed upon the sounds of each language are 1) a grammatical system, and 2) a semantic system—determining the conventional meanings attached to its words. Language is basically phonological—merely a sound or phonetic system. Only secondarily does it become semantic—establishing a relationship of meaning and sound.

The mind makes sound and meaning correlations, but only by arbitrary postulation/imposition. After a while, the connection no longer seems arbitrary but conventional: we now think meaning and sound have always been together, as they have become coordinate structures. That is the way language as communication has come about, the way it is used in prose and in everyday speech. Meaning is only an enlargement upon language's basic value, its sounds.

Thus, the language of poetry does not contravene the real nature of language.

We must also discuss the musical function of poetic language. Sound is only the start of music in poetry. Words in poetry are employed for a musical duty, that of purveying musical delight. Poetry is a theater for the ear—with language that makes love to the ear. Take, for example, Cummings' lines: "All in green went my love riding / on a great horse of gold...." That beautiful roll of musical language is what constitutes its poetry—and not its meaning. (If you converted Cummings' lines to "My girlfriend went riding in a green dress on a yellow horse," the musical excitement is gone although the meaning is pretty much the same.)

Many poets today do not sing. They croak and grunt. Their words, directed by idea, clog about on platform shoes. But in order to be a poet you must have a golden throat rather than a golden mind. Poetry refines words through music and sensory nuances. It does not brutalize them with meaning.

Poetry wants seduction by language. Music is the floor on which poets move. (Balanchine said: "... music is the floor on which dancers dance.")

A poem without music is like a ship in dry dock—it cannot navigate. A poem navigates in its real waters—music.

The closer one gets to pure poetry, discussed in Chapter 13, the more words tend to lose their meanings, while their musical values increase.

Herman Hesse explained that the function of the poet is "to sing... with ever gentler, ever finer, ever more floating sounds, so that the content of the song is more and more forgotten in the joy...of making music."

Cummings began a poem with the lines: "anyone lived in a pretty how town / (with up so floating many bells down)...." The music of these lines is like champagne bubbles rising and dancing—as meaning the words are unimportant.

Another consequence of the importance of the sound and sensory verbal values of the language of poetry is that poetry is essentially untranslatable. Translation alters the key relations of the original musical and textural sounds of poems. A translation may convey the logical meaning or semantic sense of the poem, but all poetic values disappear as the sound, of necessity, changes. Such translation can be analogized to converting a color photograph into black and white—all the figures are still there but the vibrancy and color have disappeared.

Apart from the loss of the sound values and choreographic order, the brilliance, density and weight of words cannot be translated. Nuances are lost, as words have no exact semantic equivalent in another language.

Prose, however, is translatable because it of its dependence upon meaning.

Prose language is simply lingual in the sense that it utilizes the normal and natural language of ordinary speech. However, in poetry, language is linguistic, in the sense that words are appreciated for their special values. Utilizing linguistic language, the poet explores the possibilities, joys and special characteristics of language, its sensory qualities, music, rhythms, textures, nuances, sophistries, delicacies, sounds, magic and intensity. Linguistic language is language that is activated, invigorated and electrified.

Art is always linguistic rather than lingual. When you read poems, read them linguistically, to detect their special uses of language.

## CHAPTER EIGHT

# Rhythm in Poetry

To learn to write poetry, you must learn to read good poems—by reading them in a way to appreciate their special qualities.

Another important difference between poetry and prose is in the manner of their rhythm. Rhythm is movement that has a certain regularity of rise and fall—where there is periodic recurrence of a beat, thus making a consistent musical pattern. The effect is not just undulations, but patterned and balanced undulations.

In poetry, the rhythmic unit is called a *metric foot.* This metric foot comes, so to speak, in two sizes: either in two syllables or in three syllables. The disyllabic (or dissyllabic) feet are the iamb, the trochee, the spondee and the pyrrhic, two syllables that differ depending on where the emphasis is placed. Trisyllabic feet are the anapest, the dactyl, the amphibrach, the cretic, and so forth. Again, the stress is placed differently on each of these feet. In Chapter 1, I said we would not study metrics and we will not, as metrics is nonsense foisted on poetry students by teachers who pretend to knowledge.

William Meredith said:

> "I wouldn't scan a poem while I was doing its important work...any more than I would refer to a marriage manual at a critical moment: if the instinct fails, so will the act."

Knowledge of these terminologies or nomenclatures is of no importance to the creation and actual writing of poetry. They have no practical application to the writing of poetry. They are merely high-sounding labels.

From the poet's standpoint, he has no interest in what kind of foot or meter he has used, or in what you call it. Because the meter of the poem is always *subconscious*, the poet is not aware of the meter as he writes. He is only aware of a melodic sense and of a linguistic sense and a technical sense. This is why we don't study this sort of thing.

What the poet requires is a good and fluid ear. Because he or she wants fluidity and grace of musical movement, he or she must write in the sequence of the melodic phrase—and whatever is unmusical to his or her

## CHAPTER NINE

# Organizational Differences Between Poetry and Prose

will try to define poetry and demystify it. We start by declaring that etry is a serious art, not a popular art. If you think the works of Kahlil oran or Rod McKuen serious poetry, and if the discussion of self expres-n above did not dissuade you, please read on.

Poetry is lyric poetry—poetry proper and not narrative, satiric, didactic l dramatic poetry, which, as discussed in Chapter 3, are not poetry per and are applied to the service of something other than poetry. Verse olied to the matter and uses of prose is not, strictly speaking, poetry. en you versify prose matter, it is like the music played in a movie in the kground of the actors speaking.

Poetry also is not a performing art. Many people only know "poetry" ough poetry readings. However, to expect a poem to be read aloud first order to hear the music makes little sense—it is like viewing paintings a museum with someone describing the painting in case something may ss your eye. If you have no eye for paintings and no ear for poetry, you nply are not meant for the joys of these forms of fine art.

A poetry reading makes invisible the form of the poem—and thus the em itself is invisible. A poem written or printed on the page is visible as m, therefore visible as art. Its faculty as art is precisely because it exists a perceived and visible body. Its form can be apprehended only in, and ause of, the physical structure that the poem assumes on the paper. Lose m and you no longer have an art object. Form is *always* the determinant o whether a work is art or not.

Ned Rorem, the composer: "Art concerns only 2 of the 5 senses: sight l sound. No art is devoted to touch, taste or smell." And, for art, it's either ht or sound, not both together. For poetry, as well as painting, sculpture, hitecture and dance, sight is involved. Sound is reserved only for music.

To observe the qualities of poetry, one must use one's eyes. The poem ıst be good on the page—and if it is—then it is also good on the ear. ery poem must be seen, not for its own sake (as a painting or sculpture is ear is rejected. In other words, a good poet always has a well inner ear.

For the purpose of our study, we have to refer to the met contrast poetry rhythm with that of prose. The metrical foot is of rhythm composed of only two or three syllables. Thus, w has a narrow or quick movement. Accordingly, we say that th poetry itself is narrow and quick. Verse moves in small quick u single line—each line containing several of these metrical feet

Prose also has its rhythm, but its movement is broad inste Prose moves by the slow and long undulations of the sentence

We will, in Chapters 11 and 20, study the differences rhythm of poetry and prose rhythm but we are now takin sweep. Before I can teach you how to write poetry, I must teach think about poetry. We are here and in the next chapter makin ic study of poetry—in an order and sequence that grows towa of knowledge and in terms that focus clearly. By such a proce up and build to clarity the world of poetry, so that poetry is n victim of *mistaken identity* (i.e., thought of as prose).

meant to be seen) but in order that its craft may be noticed and evaluated. For the craft of a poem resides in the way the lines are run and laid out on the page, and how these lines are turned at the line-break, and how they finally affect a stanza.

The most difficult problems confronting the poet are:

1. the problem of language,
2. having musicality in that language,
3. the problem of versification or craft,
4. the problem of tension and tone, and, *least* of all,
5. the problem of meaning.

### VERSIFICATION

This brings us to the subject of versification. It is yet another difference between how poetry is written as contrasted with prose. In Chapter 23, we will discuss versification in great depth, but for present purposes we will introduce versification as the methodology of governance of lines—the way they are laid out and spaced out on the page. In all good poetry, there is this challenge—the challenge of form.

Versification means line structure—the deliberate making of line units—where each line is technically composed so that it can go only so far and no farther—and the line cannot be any shorter either. The line as verse is structurally complete, even when the thought may not be complete. It may take several lines to complete the thought, but the structure of each line is complete.

This means that apart from the verbal craft we spoke of before (that the line is organized word by word), poetry has a line by line organization or line structure—where the line has limits. If the line goes beyond a certain point or fails to reach that point, then the line fails. The line can only be as long as is demanded by the music and the tension—otherwise the versification is wrong.

Take, as an example, Marianne Moore's opening lines in "The Fish":

"Wade
through black jade"

These lines cannot be written as: "Wade through / black jade" or "Wade through black / jade" because they fall flat and lose their tension and musicality.

Prose has no such line structure; its lines have no line limits. By derivation, the word "prose" comes from the Latin verb "*prorsus*," which means "to go straight on"—so that literally, prose means writing that goes straight on, and on, and on.

The line of prose proceeds headlong until it is stopped by the margin of the page—and there it breaks simply because there is no other recourse but to start a new line. It is merely a matter of physical expediency that makes the prose writer write a new line. But the prose line could actually go on and on indefinitely and endlessly in one straight continuous line, like an endless tape, if we had an endless sheet of paper. Prose is laid down margin to margin without design or pattern on the page.

"Verse" is derived from "*versus*," which means to turn. Poetry has versification—or structure and design of line—so that it has a patterned placement on the page. Thus, now you see that poetry has three organizations:

1. verbal structure: word by word;
2. line structure: line by line; and
3. overall structure: logic/sense—a vertical internal structure.

In all amateurs, there exists confusion between a poem and a nice thought that has simply been broken into lines without any structure. That which has line structure is called verse and that which has none is called prose.

In order to create line structure, you need to be a technical poet, and not merely an intuitive poet. When you can feel as an intuitive poet, you are only at the vestibule of poetry. Not until you arrive as a technical poet do you enter the hall of poetry itself.

Poetry and prose also differ in the development of structure. Prose has a spreading function: it undergoes ramifications from a main theme, or major theme, and branches out, like a deciduous tree in winter, into subordinate themes.

The poetic craft is more austere. It has a kind of linear growth—it grows in one direction only. It can have only one main stem of development—like the vertebral column of man—because poetry permits no subsidiary content. Poetry has only a major theme and no minor theme(s).

In poetry you defoliate—in prose, become leafy with details and description. What a compact and tidy novel will say in, say, 100,000 words, poetry can say in a poem of 50 words, or even in a line or a phrase. This is because of the internal imaginative speed of poetry, as well as its concentration of language. This is why many novels take their titles from lines of poetry—the line is simply expanded to produce a novel.

Ezra Pound wrote: "Poetry = condensation." Poetry is a little camera that can take big pictures.

All art is by nature a limiting affair. It puts a frame around experience, just as architecture puts a frame around space. The frame (the limits) is as important as what is enclosed. Within all art exists this principle of economy.

Poetry has an economy within that primal economy—it contracts inward and compresses—pulling in toward the smallest amount of space. Poetry miniaturizes, by distilling essence and ejecting all trappings. Just as compression forms diamonds, so does it form poems.

> EDGAR ALLAN POE: I maintain that a long poem does not exist.... The phrase 'a long poem' is simply a flat contradiction of terms.

## USE OF DETAIL IN POETRY AND PROSE

Both poetry and prose involve the use of detail in order to flesh out the body of the work. However, the details of prose are concrete objects, things, items—a catalog and enumeration of real, everyday objects. These may include facts such as the leaves on the street, the dress that she wears, the color of her eyes, the shape of her face, the size and color of the room, etc. Without these facts of actuality, the novel or story would be unreal—these objects and descriptions are necessary for creative prose.

Prose is built on the principle of concretization: What is universal must be made particular and concrete.

The details of poetry, on the other hand, are not actual objects or actual things, but metaphors. And metaphors are made of language. They do not exist in actual life because they are not physical objects but linguistic objects of imaginative fusion and abstraction. They are not factual reality but symbolic reality—metaphors acting through the powers of abstraction and synthesis.

Poetry fundamentally is abstract—works on the principle of abstractionism: the particular made universal. By its very nature, metaphor as the detail of poetry is removed from the world of fact and external reality.

Despite its economy and terseness and despite its absence of factual details, poetry makes no bald statements. Poetry's statements are non-literal and create overtones, undertones and reverberations. They are always rich.

The statements of prose, however—despite its length and wealth of details, are bald because they are literal. Fact is what it is—and not like anything else. One doesn't say: "Your eyes are *like* blue" but "Your eyes *are* blue" because that is the fact.

Metaphor always likens things to something else that the thing is not. "Your eyes are *like* stars" is factually untrue, as is "Your eyes *are* stars." Metaphor is built on the powers of language—on linguistics—not everyday reality.

From all we have now said analyzing the differences in organization between poetry and prose, we should see their differences in the technique of imagination used. Prose goes local while poetry goes express, directly to the main stop. Prose makes the imagination stop and linger at intermediate stops and is always playing for time—it needs time to carry itself out. In contrast, poetry makes the imagination leap, disdaining intermediate stops, and is always at the point of arrival.

### TENSION AND TONE IN POETRY AND PROSE

There is also a difference in the tension and intensity between prose and poetry.

Tension is a condition of pressure and strain, a feeling of tightness, of being pulled in; it is like a coiled spring that begs for release. Emotional intensity is strength of feeling and connotes drama, the involvement of the emotions. Tension can exist without intensity of feeling, and simply as a nervous condition.

Intensity is dramatic because it is emotional, whereas tension is only dramatic because it is physical.

Poetry must have tension—the nervous condition. In the matter of its language alone, poetry already exists in a nervous condition—its words are pulled so tight against each other—in a technical drama of words against words, a drama of sheer language. Not only in its language but in its organizational structure, the language of poetry is dramatic linguistically as mere language—even if we paid no attention to the meanings of its words. The tension in the language of the poem is carried over into the organizational structure of the poem. A good poem is built as if it were always ready to topple over should one make one false step. This is the tightrope esthetic of poetry—as if the poet were walking a wire above the ground, where he must keep a perfect balance or fall.

The prose writer never falls because he or she is always on the ground—at worst all he or she can do is stray off course. The language of prose is relaxed, limp and not in a nervous condition at all. One of the reasons I have asked you to stop reading fiction is so that you may learn to acquire the tightened tone and verbal tension of poetry. Stéphane Mallarmé: "Poetry is the language of a state of crisis."

### WHAT "MEANING" MEANS IN POETRY AND PROSE

Prose and poetry also differ in their respective concepts of *meaning*. When it comes to poetry, meaning is one of the pieties of the ignorant.

> OSCAR WILDE: There are two ways of disliking art. One is to dislike it, and the other is to like it rationally.
>
> JACQUES MARITAIN: Logical reason, the working reason, 'plays a secondary part in the fine arts.... As soon as it gets the upper hand, the work is but a *corpse* of a work of art.'
>
> T.S. ELIOT: The bad poet is usually unconscious where he ought to be conscious—and conscious where he ought to be unconscious.
>
> WALLACE STEVENS: One can do nothing in art by being reasonable.... But it is also true that one can do nothing by being unreasonable.

When you lack knowledge of art, you reduce the art of poetry to the one element of feeling or meaning. In art, it is not the intellectual reason that is at work, but the imaginative reason—the poet is after imaginative effect.

In poetry, metaphoric logic is active and goes by leaps and bounds instead of by ordinary steps.

Poetry can be as heavy and dense in meaning as prose, although that is not the aim of poetry. So far as the significance of content goes, there is not much difference between poetry and prose.

The differences lie in five points:

1. Meaning in prose is primary and essential, as discussed above. In poetry, meaning is always secondary. Meaning is the accidental power of poetry.

2. In prose, meaning arrives first—it is there beforehand, is pre-thought. In poetry, meaning is absent at first and then discovered.

3. The meaning of a novel or story is the result of dramatization of its content. The meaning in a poem is the result of dramatization of its language.

4. We read prose to get information and to know what happens next. When we read poetry, we are after the essence of language.
5. Prose has fixed content; it tends to one fixed and precise meaning. Ambiguity is a defect in prose, since it tends to blur things and cause imprecision. Poetry, however, can have variable meanings—it has an apparent surface meaning and also latent meanings. Ambiguity enriches poetry as it widens its meanings.

> PAUL VALÉRY: The subject of a poem is as foreign to it and as important, as his name is to a man. *Selected Writings of Paul Valéry*, 148 (New York: New Directions, 1950).

It is only when a poem is well-made, well-crafted, that it is truly a work of art. Then, and then only, the subject becomes important. We are evaluating the language and craft first, the art of language in verse form.

> VALÉRY: Thought is hidden in verse like the nutritional virtue of fruit. (Ibid.)

What the form of poetry provides us is a satisfying sensory experience—which, in art, is called aesthetic experience. Such experience is derived only from works of art. It arises through sensitivity to form. We have a delight in the performance of the artist as an artist, independent of the subject matter. Art as idea makes a skimpy lifebelt for art.

> GERARD MANLEY HOPKINS: Poetry is speech framed for contemplation of the mind by the way of hearing, or speech framed to be heard for its own sake (and interest) over and above its interest of meaning. Some matter and meaning is essential but only as an element to support and employ the shape which is contemplated for its own sake.

The ordinary reader does not really think of meaning in its great sense, but as simply something they can re-say in prose (para-phraseable content).

### POURABILITY AND IRREDUCIBILITY

When we started our discussion of the differences between prose and poetry, we noted that the first and most obvious difference is in how they look on the printed page. Prose exists in solid paragraphs, giving it a broad and solid look, and is usually extensive and massive. Poetry is in short lines, giving it a narrow and delicate look, and is brief and economical.

We did not pause to discuss this difference as it is too obvious. But if we analyze more carefully this simple difference in the physical looks of these two literary art forms, using our *mental* eyes, we come upon another difference between prose and poetry: the pourability of prose and the *un*-pourability of poetry. Prose is like water or any liquid you can pour into a vessel of any shape or height or width and it will adjust to the shape of the container and retain its original content and quality. But the shape of a poem affects the quality of the poem, for the shape of a poem is in direct relation to the quality of the versification. Poetry is hard matter from this perspective, with a shape that is inviolable.

"anyone lived in a pretty how town"—try to write this line otherwise!

Another difference is that poetry is irreducible—poetry cannot be converted to any other form of expression, into another way of saying. This is not only because of its tightrope esthetic but because of the finality of its form, where there is no displacement, nor substitution, nor omission, nor addition. No re-shaping is possible.

So, if we may summarize, prose and poetry differ: 1) as to aim/function, 2) magic, 3) genesis, 4) kinetics, 5) language, 6) rhythm, 7) physical and imaginative speeds, 8) organization and economy, 9) details, 10) intensity and tension, 11) meaning, 12) pourability and irreducibility. These are only the physiological or functional differences—but there are also collateral, psychological differences.

## SUBSIDIARY ORGANIZATIONAL DIFFERENCES BETWEEN POETRY AND PROSE

### 1. Essence

As regards essence, poetry can do and say what prose cannot do and say. As Marshall McLuhan said: "Poetry is the means of opening the doors of perception, on areas of experience otherwise inaccessible." Poetry also deliberately refrains from doing what prose can do—prose tries to copy and simulate reality. Where prose is depictive and descriptive, poetry is allusive and elusive because it does not try to copy and simulate reality—it is symbolic and abstract and works on the principle of the particular made universal.

Poetry is a distillation of life, not an imitation or representation of life. Poetry is essentiality and abstraction whereas prose is particularization and concretization—that is why poetry sheds description and details.

### 2. Time Element

The time element presents another difference between the two mediums. Prose exists in calendar, historic time. Poetry exists in another time zone.

Poetry exists in abstract time. It transfigures itself into a continuous and perpetual present—with a mythic live time that is universal, live time so that it is true at all times. It is what the Greeks call "*kairos*"—inner human time. Prose exists in what the Greeks call "*chronos*"—local calendar time. It may be calendar time in the future, as in Orwell's *1984*.

### 3. The Mind's Reaction

Prose and poetry also differ in the mind's reaction to them. In reading prose, the mind is passive—as when we are watching a movie. In reading poetry, however, the mind is active; poetry stops the routine of the mind because the very language and form of poetry are hurdles to undertake.

> RICHARD EBERHART: Prose makes you lazy. Poetry makes you bright.

> IN WALLACE STEVEN'S JOURNAL: 'Midsummer is the time for prose . . . You doze—and what more does prose do?' he asks.

### 4. Stopping Point

A work of prose stops at the end of the work—nothing more goes on. In poetry, the words stop, but the poem goes on, full of reverberations. There will be more discussion of this subject in the final chapter of this book.

### 5. Depersonalization Versus Personalization

In prose, self-effacement and depersonalization of the author occur, resulting in a sense of objectivity. In a novel, the author's voice should disappear. In a poem, it should appear. In poetry, one moves inside oneself, rather than outside oneself as prose makes you do.

> T.S. ELIOT: In a poem, you're writing for your own voice.

In reading a novel, you are only a spectator, but in reading a poem you are a complete participant.

### 6. Visual Appearance

The poem's optics is a presentation—because it has its special and individual figuration and design. Prose has no figuration at all.

There is an esthetic beauty and pleasure derivable from the mere visual look of the poem on the page—but, of course, not from the poems of amateurs and non-poets. Some poems are beautiful just by their looks, even if we didn't bother to read them. Marianne Moore's "The Fish" is such a poem. You can look at poetry, but in prose there is really nothing to look at. All prose has the same look, blobs of words on the page. But a poem's stanza creates a physiognomy for the poem. Each poem has its own individual pattern and design.

### 7. Re-reading

In general, prose is intended to be read once—unless you happen to be a scholar and are making a special study of the work. Poetry is for re-reading, and the more we read it the more we see in it, and the greater becomes our pleasure.

### 8. The Rules of Grammar

In prose you must adhere to the rules of grammar. In poetry, you can go ungrammatical for the sake of sound. You have heard of "poetic license."

### 9. Point of Contact

The point of contact of meaning is different for poetry and prose:

**Poetic language -> poetic meaning**

**prose meaning--- > prose language**

***Point of Contact***

V

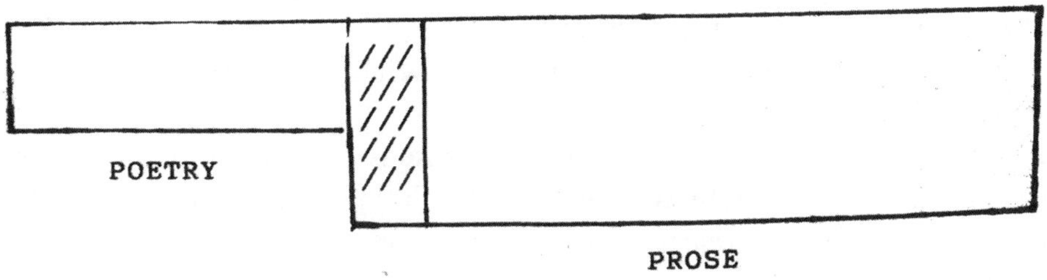

## CHAPTER TEN

# Borderline Cases

One cannot train for poetry and at the same time read and write creative prose. That would be lumping two opposing forces in one spot—it becomes imperative to separate them, to specialize.

> ROBERT FROST: You cannot sail by the North Star—when you are at the South Pole.

Poetry is not anti-prose—it is simply *un*-prose.

If you make prose values your first enchantment, your prose hangover causes trouble in the writing of poetry. Your first trouble will be language trouble because you will be proceeding by meaning. Next, technique trouble, then tone trouble, and so on.

An example of the poetic process working in prose is the Harold Pinter play: *The Homecoming*, described in *Life Magazine* as 'unorthodox': "He begins with not mapped out plot or characters. Instead he sits down with a pencil until, out of the blue, a snatch of dialogue strikes him, a string of words that evoke a situation and then suggest a sequence of events. The Homecoming grew out of a simple opening line, spoken by an old man rummaging through a drawer and asking 'What have you done with my scissors?'"

Use of the poetic process in writing prose is an anomalous use and results in prose. That is why we must take the hard line for poetry, instead of the soft line. We must reject the borderline cases.

Mixing photography with painting is an example of parameters being poorly defined. "Painterly photography," as it was called, encompassed the works of photographers who abandoned straight photography in an effort to turn the camera into a brush, to make a photograph look like a painting by abandoning the sharp focus, the already-defined details and the subtly-graded touch range of commercial photography in favor of soft focus, retouched negatives and the manipulated print. Painterly photography fell into disfavor and was itself abandoned.

The borderline cases in literature straddle two spheres—that of prose and that of poetry—which is like carrying on two love affairs at the same time. This hybridization process, when it occurs, represents a loss of discriminative power on the author's part, rather than an increased power. A good writer should know in which specific field he or she is writing.

Let us visit the stages along the road from prose to poetry:

- **Straight prose.**
- **Imaginative prose**—novel with a poetical essence but prosy in language, e.g., John Steinbeck, *The Grapes of Wrath*, or novel poetic in essence and language, e.g., James Joyce, *Finnegans Wake*, E. E. Cummings, *EIMI,* and *The Enormous Room.* These are still long pieces however, lacking the economy and brevity of poetry.
- **Short story—poetic in essence**, e.g., Thomas Mann, *Death in Venice;* Sherwood Anderson, *Winesburg, Ohio;* Truman Capote, *House of Flowers.*
- **Short story—poetic in essence and language**, e.g., Oscar Wilde, *Fairy Tales*.
- **Poetic passages in poetic language**, found in long stretches of prose, e.g., Thomas Wolfe, *Nightwood*—these are poetic lapses by the prose writer when he cannot help bursting into the poetic spirit.
- **Prose poem, or poem in prose**, set down as prose and with the rhythm of prose, but with a poetic brevity and with a poetic point or effect—still without the discipline and craft of verse because it is not in verse form.
- **Free verse**—minimum of craft and inadequate as verse (pseudo-versification)—it fools a lot of people because it looks like verse but does not have the technique of verse.[15]
- **Verse**—already technical in form—in the structure of verse, not of prose, as explained in Chapter 12 and in much greater detail in Chapter 23. However, verse is not necessarily poetic and can be used as a vehicle to carry matter expressible in prose but that can be said more agreeably and wittily in verse, e.g., Ogden Nash's popular animal verses.

---

15 See Chapter 11 for elucidation as to how Villa used the term "free verse."

- Last stop: **Poetry**—highly crafted in structure; highly crafted in language, highly charged in feeling and highly musical.

There are three ways of being poetic: 1) poetic in essence (spirit); 2) poetic in language; and 3) poetic in essence and language. The first sometimes can be right for prose because the spirit of poetry is at the heart of all art. However, the other two are not, and, of course, number 3 is poetry.

The exploitation of language is not in the field of the prose writer—poetic prose is prose in pantyhose, with beauty aids and false eyelashes.

# CHAPTER ELEVEN
# Free Verse

Free verse is to be distinguished from verse, the knowledge of which can turn you into a poet and the lack of which will leave you writing pretend poetry. What is needed that free verse lacks is the technique of versification. Free verse seeks, unsuccessfully, to mimic verse, which is the very foundation of poetry.[16]

In Chapter 9, we introduced the subject of versification, defining it as the methodology of governance of lines—the way they are laid out and patterned on the page. We noted that, in order to create line structure, one needs to be a technical poet.

---

16 When Villa speaks of "free verse," he is speaking of it in a negative sense: of "poems" that do not measure up to the standards of versification set out at length in Chapter 23, and in a larger sense, that are not formulated by the poetic process as described in Chapters 17–25.

Primarily, Villa is referencing prose matter that has been chopped into lines so as to mimic verse. Though generally assuming the form of short lines in contrast to sentences, these "poems" retain their prose identity because they are neither controlled by poetic language nor by the poet's craft of constructing the verse-line, with its tension and movement as a unit of structure. Some will construe Villa's denunciation of "free verse" as a call for return to "formalism" in poetry—also largely a negative term these days. However, that would be a misconception because Villa rejected insistence on many of the trappings of formalism (including strict attention to metrics, adherence to rigid and arbitrary forms, undue concern with imagery and necessity of rhyming) and instead advocated an organic, more-nuanced, approach to writing poetry governed by principles that, unlike rules, are flexible and non-restrictive. These principles are made to be infringed upon so long as the poet understands, and is faithful to, the overriding principle that a work of art—a poem—is not what it is about but what it is: its form and qualities of writing that make us experience the art.

Villa's admiration for works of Whitman, Gertrude Stein, and W.C. Williams, discussed in footnote 18 below, testifies to the necessity of reserving judgment on Villa's views about free verse until one grasps, from the lectures that constituted Poetry Workshop II (Chapters 17–25), what drew his ire about "poems" that fail to meet the requirements of verse and lyric poetry.

Verse is the physical structure and form of poetry. Poetry rests on two legs: language and versification. Language is its material and versification its structure. These are the two energy centers of poetry.

By contrast, free verse is skinless writing—without skin to hold in its material—an amorphous, sprawling mass of words as in self expression discussed in Chapter 2. The necessary skin—the technical control that provides the tension and compression—can only be supplied by technique. You need structure to have art—technique provides that structure.

Verse is the genuine thing—diamonds instead of rhinestones or the cut glass of costume jewelry. It is the gold, not pyrite (fool's gold).

Free verse, as the term is used in this book and defined in this Chapter, is pretend verse because as verse it is non-existent. Verse is patterned, has contours and movement that have been erected and shaped by technical control and manipulation.

> ROBERT FROST: I would as soon write free verse as play tennis without a net.
>
> T.S. ELIOT: No verse is free for the man who wants to do a good job.

What are the tell-tale symptoms of free verse as opposed to verse? You can tell free verse by its lack of form—its lumpiness, shape*less*ness and spill-over quality, generally evident on just a visual glance without even a reading. It is like a bag of water, all wooshy and squishy. In free verse, there is no pattern or balance—no *consistent* formal structure. Some stanzas are long, some short. This lack of uniformity applies to the lines as well—never balanced with one another. Free verse is without design, balance or harmony.

Free verse, therefore, is a visual deception—a mimicry of versification—because prose sentences have been chopped into short lines with no technical construction of verse. Free verse writing is writing under no aesthetic control whatsoever. Que será, será!

The free verse writer believes he is producing a poem-shaped object but is unaware of the artistic checks and balances needed to do so.

Free verse retains its prose construction—it still has the movement of prose. It generally breaks at the point of the easiest breakage—the breath divisions of the sentence. The break-off point in free verse is either the phrase or the breath. Free verse also follows the sense divisions of prose—its organization is logical organization.

Verse, on the other hand, is always technically tightened, line by line and stanza by stanza, as described in Chapter 23. The poetic line can proceed only so far and no farther, nor can it go shorter. The same is true of the stanza. Every line is in its strict place and limit—no line is out of joint.

It is the strictness of structure that creates the movement of verse—which is artificial—the artificial and arbitrary rhythm of composed art.

Free verse stanzas are really paragraphs because they end only when the unit of thought ends—that is why free verse stanzas are of irregular length. What is needed for verse is a formal unit of structure—a technical pattern—the technical and sensory divisions of form that are dictated by the requirements of versification.

A versified stanza may end with a hanging line, an incomplete sentence, which will not be completed until the next stanza or even later. A true stanza ends only when a technical stanza pattern is completed, whether the unit of thought is complete or not.[17]

Generally, there is a conflict between the oral rhythm of ordinary speech and poetic rhythm because poetic rhythm is artificially constructed. Arbitrary rhythm is the constructed break of the poetic line and its purpose is to create musical and technical tension—to prevent the lines from sagging and flattening out, from going limp and flabby. Arbitrary rhythm is rhythm in the process of tightening itself, of accenting itself by tension. It inflects the line, tenses it up, braces it up—energizes the line as writing and pulls it erect and alive.

Arbitrary rhythm is the pull of art versus the pull of natural speech rhythm. Free verse lines are dispirited and lethargic.

In poetic rhythm, the arbitrary pause may occur after the natural pause, as in Cummings' "Somewhere I Have Never Travelled, Gladly Beyond" (*Twentieth Century American Poetry*, 262), or before the natural pause, as in Wallace Stevens' "Peter Quince at the Clavier" (Ibid., 97), or may coincide with the natural pause, in which case they are syncopated rhythms. All of these occurrences can happen in one poem.

For examples of excellent versification in *Twentieth Century American Poetry*, *see* Marianne Moore's "The Fish" (172–73), John Peale Bishop's "A Recollection" (286), and Richard Wilbur's "Beasts"(488–89).

---

17 Villa cited examples of "poems" employing the oral rhythm of ordinary speech in the anthology books that he recommended to the members of his workshops (see footnote 9 in Chapter 1): In *A Pocket Book of Modern Verse*, Stephen Crane's "I Stood Upon a High Place" and "A Man Saw a Ball of Gold in the Sky," 216; Marianne Moore's "Silence," 349; and John Crowe Ransom's "Blue Girls," 350. In *Twentieth Century American Poetry*, Wallace Stevens' "Thirteen Ways of Looking at a Blackbird" and "Domination of Black," 108–111; Ezra Pound's "The River-Merchant's Wife: A Letter and Dance Figure," 145–47; and Amy Lowell's "The City of Falling Leaves," 52–55.

For a prose poem, see Carl Sandburg's "Cool Tombs" (Ibid., 73). Neither free verse nor a prose poem is in verse—they differ in lineation. Prose poems are the better of the two forms, because free verse has pretensions of being verse. Prose poems have no such pretensions, but remain prose nevertheless.[18]

---

18 Villa's condemnation of free verse comes with a *caveat*: Villa admired poems that some may argue meet his criteria for free verse. For example, Villa was a devotee of Walt Whitman because of his rhythmic and visceral approach to poetry. Villa considered that Whitman's poems transcended those of many who did not employ the craft of versification. See, for example, Chapter 18, page 102, in footnote 27, where Villa cautions that poetry should not make enumerations but qualifies that statement by saying: "Only Walt Whitman was entitled to do that." As noted on page 103, in footnote 27, Villa read the complete poems of Whitman in every year in which he was writing poems.

Some may construe Villa's stance against free verse as a condemnation of Gertrude Stein's poetry. Yet Villa opined that she "proved her genius by being serious about poetry and, at the same time, not making sense." However, he observed that she never produced a masterpiece but was a precursor of poets who did. See pages 58 and 76 below.

William Carlos Williams wrote poems that, in Villa's terms, could be characterized as free verse. Villa's only reference to Williams herein is to a comment by R.P. Blackmur at page 153, that Williams was "objectivism—without objective." Yet Villa commented to this Editor that Williams' poem "The Red Wheelbarrow" was one of his better poems. That may have been faint praise because, while the poem has a distinct and balanced pattern and can in no sense be described as "wooshy or squishy" or chopped up into uneven and unbalanced lines, it does not (in this Editor's opinion) meet Villa's other criteria for qualifying as a work of art. While verse, it is "mere verse" (see page 51 below) in that "the poetic process is not at work, since poetry is a voyage of discovery and starts with no subject matter.... Mere verse has a prose life because it depends upon meaning."

Williams himself attributed the inspiration for this poem to his affection for an old Black man and his son, in whose backyard he saw a red wheelbarrow surrounded by white chickens, acknowledging that "I suppose my affection for the old man somehow got into the writing." [Quoted in Rizzo, Sergio, "Remembering Race: Extra-poetical Contexts and the Racial Other in 'The Red Wheelbarrow,'" *Journal of Modern Literature* 29 no. 1 (2005): 35.]

In his "A Sort of a Song," Williams wrote: "No ideas but in things." This bespeaks an imagist philosophy that embraces the idea of written expression in clear, sharp, minimal words, evident in "The Red Wheelbarrow." Villa advised that imagery had little to do with serious poetry (see pages 1-2 above) and generally rejected poetry that relied on description (see page 101 below). One suspects that Williams' first line was initially his last line, suggesting again he was not working through the poetic process (see page 98 below). Still, Villa saw in "The Red Wheelbarrow" something beyond these possible criticisms. Speculating as to why, what he may have seen was that Williams' description of what he viewed in the old man's backyard went beyond mere description and was itself a metaphor for respecting the beauty of the neglected environment, on which (in the first line of the poem) "so much depends." Thus, Villa may have concluded that the poem has a dimension of meaning beyond mere meaning. See page 101 below.

Villa's pronouncement in Chapter 3 that poetry has more non-rules than rules, and that restrictive non-rules are principles that serve as guidelines of essential character so that poems are made true to their character, perhaps partially explains Villa's tolerance and even admiration when it comes to certain poems of Whitman and Williams.

I have interjected this discussion of Whitman, G. Stein, and Williams in the context of free verse to illustrate that Villa's denunciation of free verse should not be taken as sweeping away all experimentation in the formal structure of poems. A great deal of what Villa was railing against was prose masquerading as poetry, not just the pathetic efforts of the "say-something poets" who view poems as an art of subjective expression (see the Editor's Epilogue) but the more serious efforts of respected poets. Elizabeth Bishop, for example, in her poem "In the Waiting Room," violated many of Villa's injunctions, including perhaps his most important one: "If you can say it in prose, don't write it as poetry" (Chapter 18, page 100)]. On the other hand, Bishop in 1972 wrote a poem entitled "Poem" that uses prosy and prosaic language but appears to have a dimension of meaning beyond mere meaning, and she shared with Williams the view that there is a close association between poetry and painting.

## CHAPTER TWELVE

# Verse and Lyricism

### VERSE

Verse is working in the direction of poetry. Thus, poetry is what can happen to verse.

The value added in poetry, which is not necessarily present in verse, is the *lyrical spirit*. Poetry without lyricism is like chicken salad without the chicken. The lyrical spirit is the great conservation principle of poetry. It defies gravity and soars. A poem that is not lyrical is like a balloon that does not rise. The poet keeps words aloft and high flying.

Lyricism is poetry looking for itself until it finds itself, and smiles.

We have now reached the *centric view of poetry*—we will now be concentrating on *verse and poetry*. The *centric view*, which is our particular field, confines itself to the art of *literary versification* alone—to the spirit of poetry as found in the discipline of verse. If it is not in the form of verse, we disqualify it.

Essence may be poetic or non-poetic but its wrapping in a particular form is going to decide whether it is prose or verse. The moment that writing is poetic in form (as opposed to essence)—which means poetic in technique—then it would be verse.

Only the imaginative production in verse should be called poetry. To be a poet means to write in verse form. One must have the technical knowledge of what verse is.

Verse, then, let us define as the deliberately constructed physical structure of poetry. Verse is the way sentences in a poem are broken into lines—by musical and tensional necessities—and how these lines are laid out on the paper, to form stanza patterns. Verse is that special something you must do in order to be a poet. If you are using poetry as a medium, then you'll have to use poetic means—and that is versification.

When Stephen Spender first met T.S. Eliot, Spender said to Eliot: "I want to be a poet."

Eliot replied: "You mean—you want to write *verse.*"

But here's a strange thing—you may have poetry—but you may not have a poem. Why? It may not be in verse.

On the other hand: You may have a poem in verse—but it may not be poetry. Why? It may be in verse but only verse.

The truth is that—a poem may be either verse or poetry. When is poetry verse only—or mere verse? There is verse applied to the service of subject matter—where the subject matter is known beforehand and is of greater importance than the verse, for example, in the short narratives of Robert Frost. In "'Twas the night before Christmas," the poetic process is not at work, since poetry is a voyage of discovery and starts with no subject matter. This is what is called applied poetry. Mere verse has a prose life because it depends upon meaning.

Verse is structural dynamics, but lyricism (poetry) is aerial dynamics—it leaps off the page.

There is a point where poetry is *un*-poetic—that is when it is only verse. Verse is the first (but low) condition of poetry and poetry is the high condition of verse. V + L = P (verse plus lyrical spirit equals poetry). If we transpose the equation, we get V = P – L.

For examples of verse that lack the lyrical spirit, see in *A Pocket Book of Modern Verse* Robert Frost's poem "Provide Provide" (233), and in *Twentieth Century American Poetry*, Marianne Moore's poem "Poetry," which she later republished as a one-stanza poem as explained in Chapter 24.

## LYRICISM

And so we inquire: What does the lyrical spirit consist of? Edith Sitwell called the lyrical spirit "that rose the lyric." She meant the lyric has the quality of a rose—it is like a beautiful flower; the rose spirit pervades the lyric. For the same reason, Karl Shapiro calls poems "the flowers of language."

Richard Wagner has called "the lyric…the beginning and end of poetry."

A miracle occurs when the lyric spirit enters a work—the work is no longer flat, no longer at "street level"—it takes to the air and gives you a lift.

That is why the symbol of poetry is Pegasus—the winged horse that flies rather than treading along the ground.

We sense this lift even if we don't understand the poem completely. The secret of poetry's power is its lyricism.

Lyricism is not only the center of poetry—it is the point where all the other arts become poetry and meet with poetry. When we say that a painting or a novel or a sculpture is poetic, it is because they reach and touch this lyric center. Poetry is the solar system of all the arts.

The word "lyrical" derives from the word "lyre"—which was the musical instrument of classic antiquity. Therefore, the word "lyrical" stands for the element of song or musicality. In the lyric, there must be the singing line—we do not mean poetry set to music—it is the poem itself that must sing.

Lyric is not simply one category of poetry, but the whole of poetry itself. Lyrical is what all poetry is—poetry is always lyrical. A poet who is not lyrical is not a poet, but a versifier.

People think of "poetry" as an umbrella word, encompassing such content as epical, narrative, didactic, dramatic, devotional, epistolary, philosophical poetry. However, when it comes to poetry as a serious art, there is only one bull's eye—lyrical poetry.

André Gide: "One can only be an artist—on condition of mastering the lyrical state; but in order to master it, one must first experience it."

The magic of poetry is a white magic, a pure magic. It is the magic of poetry that gives pleasure.

Examples of poetry that is most lyrical—in contrast to the examples above of verse that are not lyrical—are in *Twentieth Century American Poetry* Robert Frost's poems "To Earthward" and "Fire and Ice" (69–71), and Cummings' poem "Somewhere I Have Never Travelled, Gladly Beyond"(262).[19]

Poetry can assume any form—sonnet, couplet, triolet, quatrain, villanelle, sestina, ode, canzone, or a form that has no name—so long as it has the qualities of, first, song or musicality, and second, very closely allied to this quality, is the quality of *magic*—the power of enchanting, putting the reader under a spell or incantation.

---

19 It is an interesting fact about Villa that in his workshops he never used his own poetry to illustrate principles about poetry he was teaching. This was so although he had written many beautiful poems, some about the poetic process itself, and had been responsible for many technical innovations pertinent to versification. He did, however, on occasion use his students' work for illustrative purposes. The student work that Villa probably used the most for such purposes was a "pure" poem of student George Wagner:

> butterfly
> flutter by!
> u better fly!

Villa described this poem as pure concrete poetry and noted that as content it is still practically nothing but with some human element. In the context of the lyricism of poetry, he said of this poem that it has magic, adding: "But if you used 'you' instead of 'u' (in the last line), it has no magic and is not in the medium."

Paul Valéry: "What is most powerful in original poetry: the magical formula." He elaborated: "What the reader expects of this magic is not a revelation, allied to knowledge, science and philosophy.... It is not a question of learning something, but of 'living a different life.' The reader becomes...enslaved, as by a charm, to the caprice and prestige and powers of language."

In Chapter 13, we will discuss pure poetry at length, particularly in discussing the work of Gertrude Stein, the great experimenter in language, who wrote: "A rose is a rose is a rose." That is a magical utterance. How different it is from writing: "A rose is a rose." The latter is mere statement. Other Stein utterances of similar ilk are: "What is it that water does do / It falls it does too" and "It is not easy to give a lion away / What did you say? / I say it is not easy to give a lion away." Notice the musicality of these utterances.

Lyrical spirit is directly connected with the spirit of play. The poet plays with language and sound—the poet makes beauty through the music of words, and enslaves and enchants us.

All good poets relegate meaning (subject matter) as the last factor in good poetry. Good poets insist upon the magic and music of language—and, of course, form, the form of verse. Play, we should now realize, is the very instinct of poetry, music (song) is its voice and behavior and discipline—its training that makes it art. The spirit of play is important to every artist in any field.

There are different kinds of magic that operate in poetry:

1. **Essential magic**—the purest kind, the most unaccountable for. Cummings: "Anyone Lived in a Pretty How Town," in *Twentieth Century American Poetry* (258).

2. **The magic of language.** Dylan Thomas: "Altarwise by Owl-Light"; George Barker: "Sacred Elegy: Separation of Man from God"; in *A Pocket Book of Modern Verse* (560 and 531–32, respectively).

3. **The magic of sound**—sense of musical delight. George Barker: "Allegory of the Adolescent and the Adult," (Ibid., 528–29); D. Thomas: "Especially When the October Wind," (Ibid., 556); and Cummings: "Anyone Lived in a Pretty How Town," see (1) above.

4. **The magic of concept:** imagination and originality. D. Thomas: "What is the metre of the dictionary?" in *A Pocket Book of*

*Modern Verse* (561), and "Now stamp the Lord's Prayer on a grain of rice," (563).

5. **Magic can consist of the element of charm.** Ezra Pound: "Ancient Music" (Ibid., 305); Emily Dickinson: "Immortality" and "In the Garden," in *Twentieth Century American Poetry* (13–14 and 7–8, respectively).

6. **Or a combination** of the foregoing.

A fourth quality of the lyrical spirit (over and above musicality, magic and spirit of play) is the quality of purity of grace and spirit. The lyrical spirit is a spirit of grace—it is not associated with purpose or motive, but springs from the purity of the clear human spirit. The quality of poetry is not personal, not subjectively motivated.

Although the lyric poet constantly uses the pronoun "I," we cannot accuse him of egotism—the poet's "I" is not necessarily self-referential—the pronoun enlarges and transcends the merely personal—it now becomes a mythic and dramatic "I"—what is called a "persona," greater than just the self of the poet writing. By the miracle of poetry, the "I" undergoes a transfiguration from the arrogant and self-centered "I" of personal life to a spiritual and transpersonal "I."

John Heath-Stubbs, an English poet: "I" is at the centre of the lyric poem, and only there not arrogant." He adds: "How on earth else am I to begin my poems?"

Other qualities of the lyrical spirit are intensity, and since intensity is difficult to sustain the lyric poem must be brief. Finally, the lyrical spirit must be non-novelistic and non-descriptive.

• • •

To recapitulate, the lyric spirit is the very identity of poetry, its reality principle and the proof of its legitimacy. One consequence is that poetry cannot be taught, because if the lyric spirit is not in you all you will produce is verse, which can be taught.

## CHAPTER THIRTEEN

# Purity in Poetry

Almost everything in nature is found impure—interlocked with other elements. In order to get the pure element, one has to deliberately isolate it. However, poetry and saints tend to be pure—they have a great leaning toward that quality called purity.

In the study of poetry, we are concerned with purity in the sense of the chasteness of the art without the intrusion of any foreign matter, with uncontaminated poetry in the esthetic sense of cleanliness—in terms of keeping the medium clean. Meaning or subject matter is not only a dilutant of poetry but a pollutant.

We can best illustrate this by making a Spectrum of Poetry.

When a beam of light is passed through a crystal prism, the white light fractures into its component colors and the colors will be projected into a band according to wave lengths. This band will show all of the colors of the rainbow. That is the physical spectrum—a band that stretches from violet on the extreme left to red on the extreme right.

By making a Spectrum of Poetry, we will be enabled to see the range and variegation, the latitudes, of poetry as regards contamination by subject matter. A diagram of the Spectrum of Poetry follows:

THE SPECTRUM OF POETRY

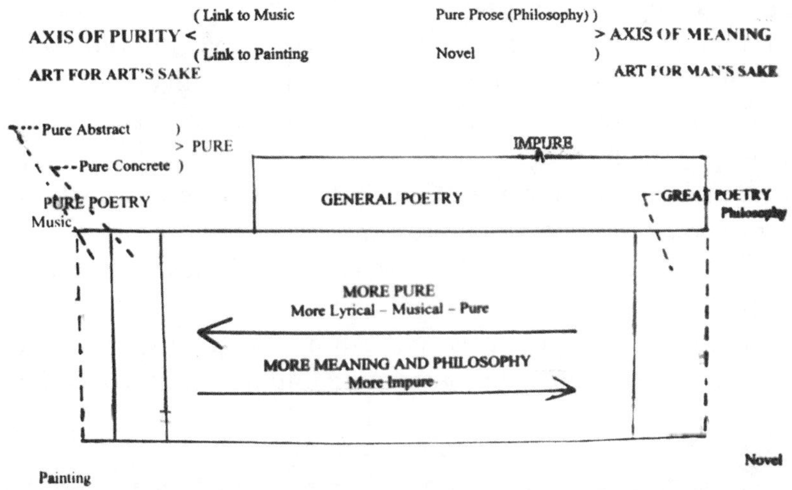

The major axis of poetry is lyricism—in pure poetry the activity is around this axis. In impure poetry, the activity turns around the axis of meaning (the minor axis), as some form of reparation or compensation for the deficiency of lyricism; it is only, as far as poetry is an art, a minor axis. Poetry's major axis will always be its lyricism.

At the opposite end of the Spectrum of Poetry is a region of great poetry—poetry where the highest meaning value is to be found. By highest meaning value, we do not mean amount of content, but weight and depth of insight. It is a qualitative depth, not quantitative.

The region of great poetry is close to God and God-like in its great humanism or what we might call art for man's sake, whereas the region of pure poetry, without content and a vacuum and therefore extremely pure, we might call art for art's sake. We have in pure poetry the purest pleasure value.

We have the noblest element of concrete humane beauty in great poetry and the highest element of abstract artistic beauty in pure poetry.

At the axis of purity with some deflection from its straight course, the art of poetry would link up with the art of music in one direction, and with the art of painting in the other direction.

At the axis of meaning, if we extended the Spectrum in a similar manner, the art of poetry would link up with philosophy (as in the works of Lucretius and Dante) and with the novel as in Mann's *Death in Venice.*

Between these two regions, we have a vast stretch—the region of general poetry—within which most poems fall, constituting neither pure poetry nor great poetry. General poetry and great poetry are both impure, i.e., poetry of content.

The Spectrum of Poetry polarizes purity and content. Here we see meaning as an adulterant and a non-poetic factor—since the poetic factors are music and magic in language. (Remember from our discussion of language that language is a system of sounds, not a system of meanings.)

In pure poetry, the medium uses itself as its sole and only source of power. The hero of the work is poetry itself, and not subject matter. Poetry is a book of magic and of formal beauty. Its ideas are not its life—its life is its authority to spellbind us.

As we move toward the axis of pure poetry, with the poetry becoming more lyrical, more musical and more pure, we are, so to speak, isolating the pure element of poetry itself, just as we can isolate the element of oxygen from impure air.

As we move toward the axis of meaning, poetry acquires more and more depth or philosophy—becomes more impure because of content.

Focusing on pure poetry in greater detail, we encounter two kinds: 1) Pure Abstract Poetry and 2) Pure Concrete Poetry.

In pure abstract poetry, every trace of impurity has been removed; there has been a complete elimination of subject matter and so now there is an abstraction from, an absence of, human motive or concern—there are no human predications at all. Its appeal is completely artistic, not humanistic.

Conceptually, pure abstract poetry is non-nutritious and non-emotive . It has no inner voice—there is a complete semantic and emotional vacancy. It has been completely disjoined from any human meaning. One can say the pure poet has a genus for empty spaces.

Pure abstract poetry is, like cotton candy or watermelon, of very little nutritional value, but still can give great pleasure, purely in the pleasure sense. Poetry is mainly champagne of language—but most people want to add an aspirin to it.

General poetry is like hot dogs and hamburgers. And great poetry is like steak, which gives the heaviest nutritional value.

Pure poetry is poetry's own power, the power that derives from poetry's energy. Oscar Wilde said: "Art never expresses anything but itself." When a poem is pure, it is centered in poetry itself.

When a poem is impure, it disperses this centrality, which is taken over by content. General poetry has more content power than poetry power. As meaning is not a function of poetry, the intrusion of subject matter—objectively speaking—clouds up and weights down the clear crystal of poetry.

Harold Rosenberg , the art critic, wrote: "Abstraction is empty art—but it is correct and clean."

Pure abstract poetry is a literary abstraction—it no longer represents anything (much like non-objective painting or sculpture). It is now simply a musical presentation in terms of language—the phonetic reality of a musical abstraction. There is a subtraction from the work of any outside reference. The pure poem is a non-representational object, like an abstract painting.

Pure abstract poetry is non-literary because it has no literary text in it. It uses no meaning but is structured completely around the music of language. What makes pure abstract poetry literature, instead of being music, is that it is still in words instead of being in musical notes. It is abstract verbal music. It can be designated pure abstract AUDIAL because it is meant primarily for the ear.

Pure abstract poetry satisfies the requirements of art, if not of life—it is not-sense but not nonsense—it is art-sense.

## PURE ABSTRACT **AUDIAL** POETRY

In poetry, the word can be independent of idea and may even get rid of the idea, as in the work of Gertrude Stein. Ms. Stein taught words to go vacant. She tried to undo the dictionary and she succeeded, creating purely sound.

It reminds one of the sign in a carpet store: "For a total esthetic involvement, remove shoes." Shoes are an insulator, so your feet do not feel the rug as much. In the same way, meaning acts as an insulator as you don't feel (experience) what makes poetry an art.

Examples of abstract verbal music can be found not only in the work of Gertrude Stein in *Geography and Plays* (Boston: The Four Seas Company, 1922), but also in the poem "Jabberwocky" of Lewis Carroll [pseud. of Charles Lutwidge Dodgson], *A Pocket Book of Modern Verse* (89–90).

Fritz Peters, a young writer, visited Gertrude Stein and reported: "She found me looking at one of her books and asked what I thought of it." He replied: "It doesn't make sense," to which she responded: "No, it doesn't make sense. That's the point."

When Ms. Stein was asked by reporters why she does not write so people can understand her, she replied: "Why don't you read the same way I write?"

Gertrude Stein's poems made not a scintilla of sense. She simply played whack with language. To try to follow what she says is like trying to follow the plot in a bowl of alphabet soup. In her poems, logic has happily departed and banished itself. Words are generally handcuffed to their meanings, but Ms. Stein broke these handcuffs.

She pried words loose from their meanings and that is an act of genius. She left the words a beautiful shell of sound only—she used words as a transparent medium.[20]

In contrast, James Joyce's associative method employed the most semantically-laden language with the greatest complexities of content, blending meanings from dozens of languages in *Finnegans Wake.*

From the moment that song assumes as its calling the expression of meaning, it leaves the realm of music and has nothing in common with it. Pure poetry allows the work to break out of its bondage of meaning, to act as a free agent on its own, so that you have poetry unharmed by content. Poetry becomes a celebration of nothing other than itself.

---

20 Villa commented to the Editor that Gertrude Stein never accomplished a masterpiece, but by abolishing meaning and bringing about purification of the language thereby she led the way to Cummings and others.

**Figure 1.** Villa used the following cartoon to illustrate the pure poet's efforts to eliminate content as a means of preserving the chasteness of the medium.

*"Just shake the tambourine, please."*

**SR/ October 21, 1967**

Regarding the subject of purity and abstraction, let us see what some fine minds have said.

Albert Guerard: "Abstract art is a quest for the strength that is in purity. It is a rejection of tainted alliances."

The American painter, Ad Reinhardt, said:

> The first rule and absolute standard of fine art...is the purity of it. The more uses, relations and 'additions' [the work] has, the less pure it is. The more stuff in it, the busier the work of art—the worse it is. More is less. The less an artist thinks in *non*-artistic terms...the more of an artist he is.

Reinhardt is saying, as regards poetry, that thinking in terms of subject matter is *non*-artistic; the poet must think in terms of the medium. Reinhardt also said: "Artists—as Artists—value themselves for what they have gotten rid of and for what they refuse to do."

Clement Greenberg, [a premier art critic of the second half of the 20th Century], in "*The New Art*," 110 (1966):

> Ever so many factors once thought to be essential to the making and experiencing of art have been shown *not to be so*, by the fact that Modernist art has been able to *dispense* with them and yet continue to provide the experience of art in all its essentials...but Modernism has not thereby lowered the standing of Leonardo, Ralphael, Titian, Rubens, Rembrandt... What Modernism has made clear is that, though the past did appreciate masters like these justly, it often gave *wrong or irrelevant reasons* for doing so.

Robert Frost, in the introduction to his *Collected Poems*, stated:

> Our problem...is, as modern abstractionists, to have the wildness pure—
> to be wild with nothing to be wild about.

John Crowe Ransom observed that the poet should address himself to a "small company of readers"; he should remember that "subject matter is trifling," that "an esthetic effect may exist by itself," that he should "care nothing professionally about morals, God, or native land," and congratulate himself that poetry has "lost its public support." This is indeed very true, certainly in reference to the field of pure poetry.

> NICOLAS CALAS: The object made by the poet or painter is one that the artist gives to the world. He is giving something *useless*—as compensation for not having worked at something useful.

**Figure 2.** Villa presented the following cartoon to illustrate certain characteristics of pure abstract poetry, the artist's purpose to give to the world something beautiful even if it may otherwise be useless.

*"It's not supposed to do anything. It's just a study in abstract form."*

Samuel Taylor Coleridge noted three stages of poetry development: 1) "the attention of the reader is directed on the subject matter"; 2) the reader is "aware of a double interest in a story for its own sake, and the way in which it is told"; and 3) "the subject matter may recede to the background; instead of being the purpose of the poem, it becomes simply a means necessary for the realization of the poem." In pure abstract poetry, language has become in effect non-language, though it still employs the words and alphabet of language. The words have become abstract and non-referential, dissociated from all context. The words are merely shells of sound, phonetic shells divorced from semantic meaning. Why? Because meaning has become unnecessary: there has occurred the banishment of meaning in the service of a new order—and that order is pure verbal music, the very principle of poetry in its ultimate spirituality. The words now cohere only musically and sensuously—a sensuous but transparent medium.

The proof of the artist, therefore, is that he can discard subject matter and, from nothing, create a work of art.

> IMMANUEL KANT: In strict art, there should be *no* purpose; art is adequacy to purpose without purpose.

> ETIENNE GILSON: First, poetry forbade itself to teach, then to say anything that might be said equally well in prose; in the process of eliminating all its non-poetical elements it has finally reached a point where it no longer says anything, but this is little matter, for its essence is safeguarded, provided it attests to man's power to create formally beautiful combinations of words; only the readers are missing.

The sense of purity we find in Gertrude Stein is not confined to literature—but has pervaded all of the arts in recent times. It is most apparent in today's abstract painting and abstract sculpture. A young boy, exposed to his first abstract painting, reportedly exclaimed: "Golly, it's a picture of paint!"

Paul Valéry wrote in *The Art of Poetry* (46):

> Absolute [pure] poetry can only proceed by way of exceptional marvels; works composed entirely of it constitute the rarest and most improbable portion of the imponderable treasures of a literature.

He added: A poem's worth is its content of *pure poetry...* (Ibid., 180)

In an 1852 letter to Mme. Colet, Gustave Flaubert reflected upon pure art as follows:

> What seems to me beautiful, what I should like to do, is a book about nothing, a book without external ties which would stand by the inner force of its style, as the earth unsupported in the air, a book which would have almost no subject or at least in which the subject would be almost invisible, if such a thing could be done.... One would establish almost as an axiom, from the point of view of pure art, that there isn't any subject, for style all by itself is an absolute way of looking at things.

**Figure 3.** You should carefully study the following poem of Ogden Nash, where the true medium of poetry, language and the spirit of word play are very much in evidence.

THE PRIVATE DINING ROOM

Miss Rafferty wore taffeta,
Miss Cavendish wore lavender.
We ate pickerel and mackerel
And other lavish provender.
Miss Cavendish was Lalage,
Miss Rafferty was Barbara.
We gobbled pickled mackerel
And broke the candelabara,
Miss Cavendish in lavender,
In taffeta, Miss Rafferty,
The girls in taffeta lavender,
And we, of course, in mufti.

Miss Rafferty wore taffeta,
The taffeta was lavender,
Was lavend, lavender, lavenderest,
As the wine improved the provender.
Miss Cavendish wore lavender,
The lavender was taffeta.
We boggled mackled pickerel,
And bumpers did we quaffeta.
And Lalage wore lavender,
And lavender wore Barbara,
Rafferta taffeta Cavender lavender
Barbara abracadabra.

Miss Rafferty in taffeta
Grew definitely raffisher.
Miss Cavendish in lavender
Grew less and less stand-offisher.
With Lalage and Barbara
We grew a little pickereled,
We ordered Mumm and Roederer
Because the bubbles tickereled.
But lavender and taffeta
Were gone when we were soberer.
I haven't thought for thirty years
Of Lalage and Barbara.

From a thirty-three year high mountain I have chosen "The Private Dining Room" because I took particular pleasure in putting it together, and because it has evoked kind words from several poets whom I admire.

OGDEN NASH

Those of you who still cannot understand how a poem that is pure and that says nothing (or at least nothing relevant), can produce music and magic and delight without relying on meaning may find this poem a complete shock to your system. You may not have known that poetry need not be meaningful or have any meaning at all—that meaning is expendable freight for poetry. If you are not attracted to pure poetry, you are allergic to poetry itself and are looking for subject matter and emotionalism.

George Moore, the Irish novelist and poet:

> Why these [pure] poems are at the heart of poetry is: ideas, thoughts, reflections become common quickly; an idea is mine today, yours tomorrow, and, the day after tomorrow it is on the barrel organ. Every ten years morality, patriotism, duty and religion take on meanings different from those they had before, and that is why each generation, dissatisfied with the literature that preceded it, is inspired to write another literature round the new morality, the new patriotism, the new duty, the new religion, a literature which seems to the writers more permanent than the literature their fathers wrote, but which is destined to pass away as silently.

George Bernard Shaw's plays continue to live not because of his ideas, but because of his fascinating characters and the wonderful eloquence of their speech.

> CLIVE BELL: In proportion as art becomes purer, the number of people to whom it appeals gets less. [Because] it cuts out the romantic overtones of life which are the usual bait by which men are induced to accept a work of art. [The pure work appeals]...only to the esthetic sensibility, and that in most men is completely weak.

> T.S. ELIOT: The chief use of 'meaning' of a poem, in the ordinary sense, may be...to satisfy one habit of the reader to keep his mind diverted and quiet, while the poem does its work upon him: much as the imaginary burglar is always provided with a bit of nice meat for the house-dog.

> JACQUES MARITAIN: The point is that art stands in a line that is not the line of man's good. From this comes its strength; it is free of the human...art has for its end only the object it has chosen.

That object is *formal beauty.*

### PURE ABSTRACT **VISUAL** POETRY

There is another kind of pure abstract poetry, which we will refer to as pure abstract VISUAL—the pure poem, as a picture, seen by the eye, and linked to the art of painting. The poem has now become a visual object. It may even be wordless, i.e., contain no words at all—and just be typographic—making typography its last linkage to the art of literature.

**Figures 4 and 5.** The following works of Alan Riddell, an Australian printmaker and poet now deceased, are illustrative:

# THE AFFAIR

BY
ALAN
RIDDELL

```
i i i i i i i i i i i i i i i i i i i i i
i i i i i i i i i i u i i i i i i i i i i
i i i i i i i i i u u u i i i i i i i i i
i i i i i i i i u u u u u i i i i i i i i
i i i i i i i u u u u u u u i i i i i i i
i i i i i i u u u u u u u u u i i i i i i
i i i i i u u u u u u u u u u u i i i i i
i i i i u u u u u u u u u u u u u i i i i
i i i u u u u u u u u u u u u u u u i i i
i i u u u u u u u u u u u u u u u u u i i
i u u u u u u u u u u u u u u u u u u u i
i i u u u u u u u u u u u u u u u u u i i
i i i u u u u u u u u u u u u u u u i i i
i i i i u u u u u u u u u u u u u i i i i
i i i i i u u u u u u u u u u u i i i i i
i i i i i i u u u u u u u u u i i i i i i
i i i i i i i u u u u u u u i i i i i i i
i i i i i i i i u u u u u i i i i i i i i
i i i i i i i i i u u u i i i i i i i i i
i i i i i i i i i i u i i i i i i i i i i
i i i i i i i i i i i i i i i i i i i i i
```

**Alan Riddell**

# Just a Passing Shower

| | | |
|---|---|---|
| sunshine | sunshine | sunshine |
| sunshine | sunshine | /////////// |
| sunshine | /////////// | sunshine |
| /////////// | sunshine | sunshine |
| sunshine | sunshine | sunshine |

Pure abstract VISUAL—which is pictographic or pictorial—is what is today labeled "*CONCRETE*" poetry, a misnomer because the poetry is not concrete but abstract, except for the figure or image that it presents. Most of the general poetry that you read is more concrete.

Pure abstract AUDIAL is purer than Pure abstract VISUAL because the latter, by presenting an image, may create an idea or point.

### PURE CONCRETE POETRY

In pure concrete poetry, the content that creeps into the poem is absolutely minimal. There is only a kiss, you might say, blown to subject matter, but nothing further.

The pure concrete poem is not completely pure because there is already an acknowledgment of subject matter but it is—as Ivory Soap used to advertise—99&44/100ths percent pure. It is mostly music still, mostly song, but with some human feeling.[21]

---

21 Examples of pure concrete poems in the anthologies recommended by Villa are, in *A Pocket Book of Modern Verse*, D. Thomas, "Poem in October" and "Fern Hill"(566, 569); W.H. Auden, "Lay Your Sleeping Head My Love" (476); George Barker, "Sonnet to My Mother" (529); and A.E. Housman, "Loveliest of Trees, the Cherry Now." (159); and in *Twentieth Century American Poetry*, Wallace Stevens, "Sea Surface Full of Clouds" (111); and Delmore Schwartz, "*Mentrechè il Vento, Come Fa, Si Tace*" (349). Villa also mentioned

Pure poetry is intransitive poetry—it does not need to pass on to something else but begins and ends as itself.

JACQUES MARITAIN: "It is enough for poetry to be poetry for it to amaze."

Pure poetry, like pure science and pure painting, is good for nothing except that it is an intellectual joy.

---

three of the songs of William Shakespeare: "Spring" in *Love's Labor Lost*, act 5, scene 2; "Under the Greenwood Tree" in *As You Like It*, act 2, scene 5; and "A Lover and His Lass" in *As You Like It*, act 5, scene 3.

## CHAPTER FOURTEEN

# Great Poetry

At the opposite end of the Spectrum of Poetry (see the diagram in Chapter 13) from the axis of pure poetry is the region of great poetry, the one depicted as the region of poetry most impure because the highest meaning value is to be found there. In the region of pure poetry—to which we have just made an extended visit—we noted that we see meaning as an adulterant and non-poetic factor, as the poetic factors are music and magic in language. However, we also noted that in the region of great poetry is to be found the poetry God-like in its great humanism, or what we might call art for man's sake; alternatively, we might call it art for mind's sake.

We also clarified that, when we say that the region of great poetry has the "highest meaning value," we do not mean the greatest amount of content, but the greatest weight and depth of insight, and that this is a qualitative depth and not a quantitative one.

Although a poem is not divisible into separate parts since all of its qualities are interrelated and are inseparable coordinates of one another—existing in one solid organic whole—for purposes of study and analysis we may partition a poem's qualities into:

1. *Internal, or essential, qualities*—embracing those qualities that appertain to the intensity of the poem because these qualities spring from the interior of the poem; and

2. *External, or technical, qualities*—embracing those qualities which belong on the outside of the poem, such as the control of language and structure.

The external qualities are the ones most difficult for the untrained reader to perceive and appreciate. They can only be discovered, appreciated and savored by reference to the principles of poetry presented in this book. In any art, it is always the external qualities that are hidden and lost to untrained eyes. Consequently, people who do not see these external qualities do not see the work of art at all.

In general, the internal qualities are magic, imagination, tension, emotion, clarity and focus, originality, and—at the bottom rung of the ladder—meaning. The external qualities of poetry are its language, music, versification, economy and total form. Meaning remains at the bottom rung when the internal and external qualities are combined in the poem.

Great poetry intends only to be art and yet, from merely aesthetic imagination, it flowers and transfigures itself to moral imagination and moral radiance. In other words, the great aesthetic intelligence also becomes moral intelligence.

We can think of pure poetry as light aircraft and great poetry as heavy aircraft. Great poetry asks deep questions of mankind—questions that simply will not go away. Great poetry leads to a larger context. Richard Eberhart's great poem, "The Groundhog," in *Twentieth Century American Poetry* (350), is an excellent illustration of this genre.

The great poet writes an internal memorandum, because he writes from internal space, not outer space. The message of great art, said Rainer Maria Rilke, is "You must change your life." Art does not moralize but it can be ethical.

Meaning nevertheless is only a participatory element in great poetry; the main elements still are lyricism and craft. Although meaning is not the function of poetry, rather its malfunction, very fortunately in great poetry it can malfunction very well.

The best definition of poetry—when it is pure—is magical song. However, since poetry is seldom pure and almost always impure, the best definition of poetry that is impure is memorable speech (Auden's definition). If that definition is shifted slightly in emphasis to noble speech, then we have moved into the realm of great poetry. The meaning of the noun (speech) remains unchanged; however, the change in adjective (to "noble") requires not only speech that is memorable (the quality of being impressive in the way something is said) but also the quality of the noble or the heroic spirit.

The shift is not merely adjectival but contextual: we are now demanding great significance of meaning. For we see now that meaning—which makes poetry impure—can also make poetry truly great. In great poetry, there is always an enlistment of the spirit.

Pure poetry, you might say, is that point of the Spectrum where the Angel of Poetry commits suicide—by not being human at all. Great poetry, on the other hand, is that point of the Spectrum where the artist himself is liable to commit suicide for forgetting art—by his or her servitude to the interests of the human spirit.

Pure poetry is high art, with no connection with the spirit; great poetry is great art, which cannot exist without the spirit.

Art, when considered for itself alone, is not ethical; it requires no ethics. Poetry—when considered as an art only—in intention is non-humanistic: it only wants to be art and nothing more. Yet, in the end, in great poetry, it becomes not only an art but greatly human and God-like. Thus, although art is not ethical by nature—great art is always ethical.

In great poetry, the lyric spirit (which is simply magic and song) becomes happily stalemated by meaning; they strike a harmonious balance.

This all comes with a *caveat*: In great poetry, the meaning must generate itself from the verbal and musical development of the poem. It must be a subconscious arrival by the poetic process. Meaning becomes bedrock—because it grows out of the linguistic poetic process itself. You can have a work of art without meaning, as in pure poetry—but meaning alone cannot make a work of art—it is always the form that accomplishes it.

In the criticism of literature, the first test to apply is always the test of form, of craft—and the performance of the writer as writer should be the first pleasure for the reader. If the work is ill-crafted, it gives no pleasure and is not art. However, if the work passes the test of form, the second important test is the test of substance—of the work's human significance. This is the secondary pleasure for the reader, sharing in the experience of man as found in the work. Between two works of equal technical merit, the work that affords the deeper human experience is superior. As the human significance increases, the work travels higher on the ladder of literary greatness.

In *A Pocket Book of Modern Verse* is George Barker's poem "Sacred Elegy: Separation of Man from God" (531), which is just loaded with meaning, but poetry by meaning through language. Dylan Thomas' poem "Altarwise by Owl-Light" (Ibid., 560), is also laden with meaning, in contrast to his poem "Especially When the October Wind," (Ibid., 556), which is not.

In the great poem, the poet did not intend to say what he has said. Even without the intention to say anything, the fineness and depth of his or her life and character have evoked and elicited this great meaning. The meaning was pulled out of the poet by the writing of the poem. It is the life-force, the push of the whole man or woman shining through.

A poet's greatness, therefore, is involuntary: in the great poet, the great thoughts are produced by the poetic process—mined out of the poet's deep resources and distilled and lighted by art. The thoughts contained in great poetry do not spring from the rationality of the mind, but from the fire of the human spirit.

Heretofore, I have devalued meaning—yet, one cannot have great poetry without it. The reason I have devalued meaning is that, until you have learned a sense of language and form, you're not ready for content at all.

Art is judged always by its form and substance, what the Greeks called "*poiema*" and "*logos*." Poiema refers to the exteriority of poetry—to the visible poem with its technical and sensory organization. The poem as logos, on the other hand, refers to the interiority of poetry, to the invisible poem—its intellectual and spiritual charge. The poiema displays the technical drive and mastery of art—the triumph of organization and structure—the physical truth of the poem. The poiema makes manifest the power of art and is, therefore, the proving ground of art. It attests that the poet is an artist.

The logos displays the dramatic drive and mastery of life—the triumph of the theme. The logos reveals the poet as human and attests to the passion of his or her spirit. In the logos are the human values, the poem's human dimension.

We may compare the poiema to a beautiful rainbow and the logos to a pot of gold at the end of the rainbow. But we should always remember that the thrust of the art comes from the poiema, because it is the poiema that is the primary pleasure-giver. And if the poiema—the esthetic experience—is absent, logos is nowhere, as it can only articulate itself in and through the poiema.

In great poetry, the poiema and logos exist in solidarity and provide a double-edged experience, whereas in pure poetry one has only a single-edged experience. However, it bears repeating, because poiema is the primary universe of art and logos only a secondary universe, art is not what it overtly is about—subject matter—but about the poiema. Art desires only to be art. The good poet is more concerned with the rainbow than with the pot of gold.

The logos cannot be taught—everything depends on the kind of human being who writes the poem. He or she cannot take lessons to improve his or her logos. Poiema, however, can be taught and learned if people have enough interest and patience.

Lyricism is ethnic to poetry; it is poetry made by poetry's own driving power. The lyric spirit cannot be taught. Verse can be, but it takes a long time to master.

What does greatness consist of? 1) greatness of mind, thinking; 2) greatness of spirit; and 3) greatness of performance—which makes the poet an artist. The first quality we do not expect of the poet. The latter two are expected of the great poet—they make the great poet.

A great poem has the additional purity of the human spirit—it is pure in its conception because it started without subject matter and it is pure also in the human spirit that comes into it and pervades it.

In our diagram of the Spectrum of Poetry (Chapter 13), the regions of pure poetry and great poetry are presented as the limits of poetry—that is why they are positioned at the opposite terminals of the Spectrum. And yet both of them constitute the realm of great poetry. Is there a discrepancy there? Why do they stand so far apart?

**Figure 6.** The spectrum of poetry is not a straight, flat course, but forms a ring as portrayed in the following diagram:

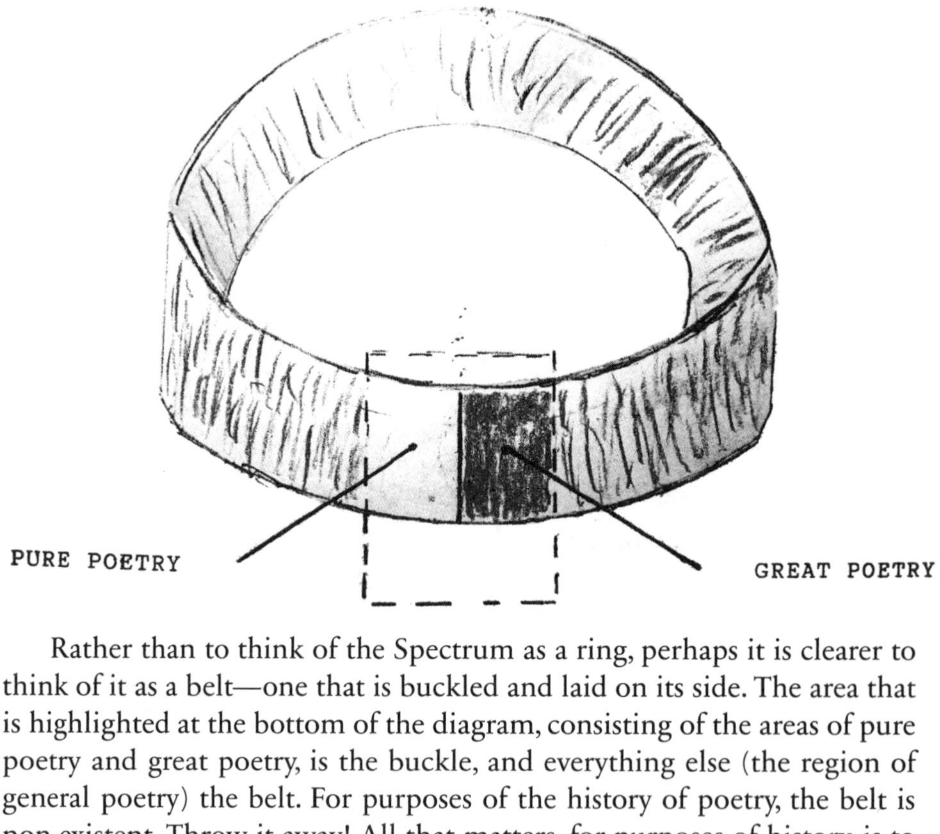


Rather than to think of the Spectrum as a ring, perhaps it is clearer to think of it as a belt—one that is buckled and laid on its side. The area that is highlighted at the bottom of the diagram, consisting of the areas of pure poetry and great poetry, is the buckle, and everything else (the region of general poetry) the belt. For purposes of the history of poetry, the belt is non-existent. Throw it away! All that matters, for purposes of history, is to be found on the buckle. Only the poets who wrote the poems represented by the buckle have tenure. It is as the Bible says: "Many are called but few are chosen."

Great poetry falls into two categories:

1. Great poetry proper or great major poetry—great by reason of its spiritual vitality, its deep humanism, its quality of serious passion, its great sense of living, its grandeur and sublimity, its vision and illumination and its sense of wisdom—such poetry is called metaphysical poetry, which is the Aristocracy of Poetry, what we may also call the Literature of Power.
2. Great poetry lyric or great minor poetry—great simply by craft and sensory beauty because of its beauty of expression and form—such poetry we call the Literature of Beauty. These artists—very good ones—produce art that leaves us thinking admiringly only of art, without making us contemplate the mystery of human life.

There is what may be called a third category of great poetry—these are the historically-significant works. They are so called not because they are intrinsically significant, but because they have created a new mode of consciousness and influenced other works, and have given direction to a body of literature. They are pacemakers and precursors, but they are "great" by concession and courtesy only. We might call this category the Literature of Direction, and some of the poets who may fall in this category are T.S. Eliot, W.H. Auden, William Wordsworth and John Keats.

Great poetry is always metaphysical because, as Coleridge said, "Genius is by nature metaphysical." Metaphysics is that branch of philosophy that treats of first principles (the science of being and becoming—the principle of selfhood and identity) and of this selfhood's relation to man and the universe—the selfhood, identity and cosmological reality of man. Therefore, great poetry is trans-physical in that it goes beyond the merely physical into abstract truth, the inner reality. Metaphysical poetry can be concrete—art that deals with the human condition and involves us with feeling through the route of intelligence—or abstract or intellectual—art that detaches us from feeling and provokes reflection instead, dealing with intellectual concepts of abstract truth and partakes of the scientific, like geometry but without the direct logic of geometry.

The dramatic power of great poetry comes from the element of agony and angst. Robert Frost: "There is a pang somewhere that makes poetry." Great poets speak out of the maelstrom of the spirit, as does the poetry of Gerard Manley Hopkins and John Donne. In them, there is not only a presence of spirit, but the conflict and expense of spirit. You can see and feel the spirit being consumed. Tolstoy wrote: "One ought only to write when one leaves a piece of one's flesh in the ink-pot each time one dips one's pen."

Nietzsche: "Of all that is written I love only what a man has written with his blood."[22]

• • •

This concludes the materials covered in Poetry Workshop I, where we have studied how to approach and understand poetry. I have tried to teach you where to focus your attention and how to make the appropriate esthetic response—to read the writing first and not the content—and that poetry is surfing the medium by the energy of language and craft. Should you choose to continue your studies, we will in Poetry Workshop II [the remaining chapters of this book] study the principles of technique: how to write the writing and how to create aesthetic effects.

---

22 Examples of *great poetry* are to be found in the anthologies recommended by Villa as follows (in no particular order): in *A Pocketbook of Modern Verse,* Eberhart, "The Groundhog" (457); Hopkins, "The Windhover" and "No Worst, There is None" (141 and 139, respectively); Owen, "Strange Meeting" (380); Whitman, "I Saw in Louisiana a Live Oak Growing" (27); Dickinson, "The Soul Selects Her Own Society," "My Life Closed Twice Before Its Close," "I Felt a Cleavage in My Mind," and "After Great Pain a Formal Feeling Comes" (77, 78, 79, and 89, respectively); Edith Sitwell, "Heart and Mind" (320); also in *Twentieth Century American Poetry*, Dickinson, "The Chariot" (5); and Frost, "To Earthward" and "Fire and Ice" (69 and 70, respectively).

## CHAPTER FIFTEEN

# Wrapping Up on Poetry's "Internals"

The only way to write good poetry is to have knowledge of both the internals and the externals of poetry. Knowledge of the internals must come first—much of what is needed we gained from the prior chapters. However, before we proceed to study technical knowledge, there is still some learning that pertains to the poetics of poetry's inner logic—pertaining to poetry's interior side, to its inner motivation and psychology—its "endo-poetics"—that was too recondite and specialized to be handled in the prior chapters and must be covered.

Thus, in this chapter and in the chapter on poetic language that follows, in addition to further discussion of the nature of the poetic process, we will cover specifically the subjects of 1) how meaning arrives by way of the poetic process, 2) expressiveness in poetic writing; and 3) the ways in which poetic language differs from the ordinary language of prose—becoming the language of the art of speech.

The creative writer is not really a thinker, in the way that a philosopher or a scientist is a genuine thinker. Thinking is not the business of the poet. His or her business is language and form and insight. And insight is not thinking at all, although it may be very great indeed.

Thinking is the difference between what went on in Newton's mind when it reacted to the fall of the apple and the reaction of all other men previously to the same situation. Newton's mind worked to determine *why* the apple fell, and he discovered the principle of gravitation.

When a poet chooses a particular combination of words because they make a better poetic effect, that makes poetic sense, but it is not thinking in the true sense of the term.

Making sense in life or in art is intelligential rather than intellectual. Intelligence is simply a sense of rightness, even when you do not know the reason you are right in what you sense. And a man can be illiterate and yet be intelligent.

The arts do not require intellect but simply intelligence. To be intelligent is to proceed rightly by innate perception, by intuitive sense.

To be intellectual, on the other hand, is to proceed by cultivated reasoning. Intellect is a more specialized faculty than intelligence. Intelligence proceeds only by general perception rather than analytic endeavor. To be intelligent is to know, but to be intellectual is to know why. Intelligence knows quicker than intellect, as reasoning and analysis take time. The ideal mind is one that works by both powers.

An intellectual mind is always an idea mind. Artists, being mainly intuitive and sensorial, are generally not idea minds.

The problems of art, therefore, may be resolved by intelligence; intellect is not needed for their solution. It requires no intellect to know that water quenches thirst.

Ned Rorem, the composer, on receipt of an invitation from Buffalo University to deliver lectures, confessed: "I was uneasy.... What did I know about music except writing it? For the first time I was required to consider my craft without using my ear." His uneasiness arose from being asked to use his intellect.

### HOW MEANING ARRIVES IN ART AND POETRY

Most people, confronted with a poem, want to know what its meaning is. Back of this content obsession is the fact that they are unaware of the difference between content and meaning. Content is anything contained in a receptacle, like fruit contained in a bowl, but even if the bowl is empty it still has air content.

Literature, being a verbal medium (and words generally carry meanings), usually has a positive content, or sense—but on the other hand it may hold a negative content or not-sense as in Gertrude Stein's experiments with language. But even the not-sense of Gertrude Stein is content, in the same way there is air content in our fruit bowl. So, such a poem still has content although it may not be recognizable because it is not logical.

As it is, the ordinary reader only looks for recognizable content, and so long as he recognizes something he can understand he feels that the poem is justified—even if the poem is not significant at all.

This is the point at which meaning enters. Meaning has a connotation of significance—it is not just to say something that is understandable, but to say something of import. Where import is lacking, there is really no meaning, just content.

In philosophy and in the intellectual sciences (e.g., history, economics, chemistry, mathematics, criticism), meaning is directly stated. In art and literature, however, meaning is not directly declared.

In art, a word is "expressive" and effective not because of what it says in the semantic or logical sense, but because the word has the capacity to evoke and cause a response in the beholder—through the expert and effective use of the medium.

What a work of art "expresses" cannot be verbalized in words, because what it expresses is non-verbal, "non-wordable." It is the medium itself that is now speaking, the presence and aliveness of the medium that makes the work expressive, and not the logical content.

Thus Marshall McLuhan declared: "The medium is the message." The content is not the meaning of the work. The message is what the medium does whatever its content may be, and its content may be positive or negative sense.

Thus in poems where the subject matter is the sole purpose of the writing—where you have literal brute content—you have no poem because it should be the medium that is active. Every good artist must have a sense of the medium in which he is involved.

Sense of the medium in poetry means to explore the resources and values of the medium of language—to enjoy its sensuous, physical properties and to discover their technical possibilities. The values involved are sensory and technical, not semantic. The course of action in a poem is in the maneuvers of language itself. The medium is different from what it handles, which is content.

When we hear a song being sung, we realize that the voice is different from the words of the song and different from the song or melody. Although the words may be good, the voice may be terrible (or magnificent). The words are the message; the song the formal structure; and the voice the medium. Therefore, the message is the least important; and the voice the most important.

The medium is the line of transmission, the conduit, but not the content itself. Each medium is different in that it has its own limitations, as well as its own special abilities. You cannot expect the sound of a violin to emerge from a piano, or a trumpet or flute, although they may be playing the same music. The melodic structure is not the medium.

This means that there is an immediacy of effect possible only in the particular medium involved. It has unique effects available only in that medium, peculiar and very exclusive to itself. One medium cannot substitute for another.

When ballet is converted into film, as was done in the film *An Evening with the Royal Ballet*, featuring Rudolph Nureyev and Dame Margot Fonteyn, the New York Times film critic, Bosley Crowther, wrote: "But it cannot escape the inevitable inconsistencies of filmed stage ballet, which reveal the embarrassing conflict of the aesthetics of the two art forms. The complex and flowing composition of the choreographers are smashed every time the film director cuts from a long shot to a close [shot]." In other words, the media are not interchangeable.

It is the same thing with prose and poetry. As they are two entirely different media, we should not expect of poetry what we expect from prose, and vice-versa.

When you know what a particular medium can do, or will not do, and when you can use this knowledge to enrich and control your medium—when you can show not only what is possible with the medium but stress those things that can be done only in that medium—then you have a sense of the medium.

Thus, in the medium of poetry, you can banish meaning (G. Stein), attain deepest meaning (Eberhart), make different kinds of music, make a painting, recreate the very spirit of things, accelerate motion (Cummings in *Buffalo Bill's*) while working within the resources of the medium. That does not mean limiting or circumscribing oneself, as the medium may surprise you with a new faculty it has not shown before.

When you think of language as a medium, you think of abstract relationships of words, i.e., disconnected from their meaning. Sound and texture are the greater medium for art. Meaning is simply the smaller medium within this grouping.

In a work of art, therefore, it is the medium itself that does its own thing—the medium was made expressive by the author's skill, and not by the content of the work. It was the author's know-how to understand and respect the nature of the medium and to tackle and exploit its resources. The medium has been given an immediate life and acquired a presence and impact that are much more than the literal content it holds and presents.

The medium is concerned with effect involving the total situation, whereas the content involves only a simple level of the total effect. When the medium is effective, the content is also effective. When the medium is not effective, the content has no effect, as the subject matter only comes alive when the medium is alive. Reminds one of the song: "It don't mean a thing if it ain't got that swing."

Content, then, is only the medium within the medium—the medium for meaning within the greater medium of form.

## EXPRESSIVENESS

Where language is merely literal, directly expressing the idea (e.g., "Life is painful"), there is no expressiveness. It is only after long practice, and long training with language, that one attains true expressiveness. When Shakespeare, in one of his songs, writes "With a hey, and a ho, and a hey nonino" (*As You Like It*, act 5, scene 3), although these are not-sense syllables, they are more expressive than "Life is painful."

When a statement is "expressive," it does not mean that it contains great or even important content, but that the manner of expression is effective by its special way of treating the point. To be expressive, you play language on itself; from the play of language results a play of ideas. You do not start with idea and go into language. Examples are: "Male Basset would like to meet female Basset—Object: Bassinet"; "Where to stop the escalation of milady's dress is developing into a new battle hem of the republic"; "Is there too much month at the end of your money?"

Expressive writing is not the mere uttering or declaring or asserting of an emotion or thought—the true artist utters less, but evokes that feeling or thought more. And he does this by producing effects, by developing literary qualities, through technical and sensory devices, verbal balance, a sense of language mingled with craft.

The words of language come to us expressionless in their natural state and their ordinary condition. It is necessary to harness the words of language in order to release their energy and power. That is what the poet does. He tightens words so that there is pressure, activates them so they are completely active inside and out, so that they crackle and sparkle.

Expressiveness is what Dylan Thomas called "the color of saying" (ordinary speech is colorless).

> VIRGINIA WOOLF: Writing needs screwing [tightening] of the brain.

True expression, then, is the squeezing out of values from words and is very difficult even for good poets.

# CHAPTER SIXTEEN
# Poetic Language

Language is what is happening in poetry. The action is in the crafting of poetic language by the poet's technique. To use Dylan Thomas' phrase: this is "the green fuse that drives the flower."

Poetry is delight—the manipulation of language to produce special effects.

Language is the very first reality of poetry, as technique is its second reality, and its ultimate reality: lyricism and insight. You need all three to make fine poetry—the trinity of language, craft and insight. Poetry is at the intersection of lyricism and craft, built on language.

Good poets make words better than they are in the dictionary. The good poet's language doubles back on itself, surprises the poet and surprises the language itself.

The poet gives primacy always to sensory values of words, because what he is involved with is not speech itself but the art of speech.

In a poem, each word has to be right and to contribute to the whole.

As discussed in some detail in Chapter 7, language in ordinary speech and in prose is semantic only—thought is the only thing transmitted and the language itself has no powers. In prose, it is the content that holds the power. Consequently, prose has the pulsation of meaning only, whereas poetry has the pulsation of language itself.

Poetic language is language plus, or language plus and special effects. Poetic language has verbal, sensory and symbolic values. Poetic language is tight in construction because it is based on verbal and sonal balances, on verbal nuances, as well as the technique of verse. So it is full of verbal surfaces as well as verbal depths.

Poetic language has an open logical system because it employs metaphors. "A black white" becomes metaphoric in poetry, where in prose it would be nonsense.

Poetic language needs not only encoding but decoding. Because of the transition from common-sense speech to art speech, alterations and shifts of attitude and even meaning occur.

The poet disrupts and dislocates ordinary language. Even a slip of the tongue: "My baby is going to have a wife"—which reverses the order—upsets the routine order and routine expectancies and creates greater force.

In poetry, the words are not mere signposts of their meaning—they are enactors of the meaning. For example, Cummings' "anyone lived in a pretty how town" where the floating is enacted by the language.

By the way the poet uses words he is creating another language altogether—a linguistic language within lingual public language—a language of sensory complexes rather than ordinary language.

In poetry, language is not only medium but also material. Poetry uses language in two ways: 1) as material, primarily to convey the sensory joys of language, and 2) as medium, secondarily to convey meaning. That is why poetic material is rich, dense and sensuous, while prose material is weak and pallid.

The difference between material and medium is a special difference that particularly enables poetry to behave as poetry, while prose remains mere prose. Material is the corporeal, physical substance of which a thing is made, the organic and concrete being of anything. It is tangible and physical, not an abstract intellectual quality but a sensory physical reality.

Air is the common medium for sound. Without air, sound would not be transmitted. But air is not the material of sound because sound is not made of air.

The medium is simply the conduit, a means for transmittal, like wires that carry electricity. Electricity is not made of wires. So the medium is different from what is carried.

Where the carrier and the carried are one and the same in action and identity, then you have material—as language is said to be the material of poetry—the poetic tissue.

Language used as material results in verbal texture, endowing the poem with a sensory and active surface, turning the language itself into a creative force. Language in full creative force is the material of poetry.

Now you should understand better why Marshall McLuhan said: "The medium is the *massage.*" The language is massaged, from medium into material in poetry.

In poetry, words are used visually, typographically, texturally, musically, tensionally—to create a percussion fabric, so that the poem is a sensory thriller all the time as it proceeds. It creates a verbal, tactile, sonal web of values, where you may feel the very magic and flesh of language.

Words, by themselves, are merely sensory, not musical, but when combined with other words they create a musicality. Therefore, the first clearance a poet must make, in order to admit a word to a poem, is sensory. Such a combination of words is called felt language. Felt language is language felt first by your sensory system, not by your emotion or mind. "Felt language" has to be felt by your sensory system, not by your heart. If you refer to a girl in her dress, your choice of language is vulgar, and lacks sensation. However, if you refer to a girl in her "she-shell," this formulation is sensuous and no longer vulgar.

The sensory aspects of a word are:

1. Its physical and visual look: its size (long/short), its shape, its weight and texture—whether it looks smooth or rough, airy or dense, fat or thin, light or heavy, opaque or translucent;
2. Its sound—harsh or soft, sharp or blunt, full or hollow, round or sharp, heavy or light;
3. Its time duration—which depends on its length and length will make a word dominant and more emphatic but will also get involved with the poem's rhythm; and
4. Imagistic aspect—the image it conjures forth, which must tally with previous images.

All good poets—e.g., D. Thomas, Cummings, Stevens, Donne, Hopkins—made productions out of language—in poetry we magnify the situation called language. It is this production that is the art-language of poetry.

A poem is made of word complexes. Poetry uses words as if they were chemical atoms—you must expect explosions and implosions—attacks as well as rebounds. For each poetic word is like a magnetic field, and when it meets another word there is a sudden, violent contact between them, a percussion. It is this action of sensory qualities that makes the medium swing and the medium in this swinging condition is called poetic tissue. Thus the poetic word, unlike the prose word, is not tied to one meaning but has multiple meanings. The poetic word is free and resonating, continually vibrating resonances. The movement of words in poetry must become material in order for it to be poetry.

Employing the medium as material—movement that is sensory, textural, musical and technical—requires a poet.

The words of poetry, after being used, escape forever and are not re-usable. This is so because, even if the same word is re-used, it is no longer the same word. It has gathered another new and delicate force. For example, every time Cummings used the word "rose" in his poems it was no longer the same word but had undergone a transformation into a new and special sense.

But words to a prose writer can be captured and stored in a reservoir to be captured again, for they will always have the same (usual) meaning.

| | |
|---|---|
| ROBERT FROST | Poetry consists of words that have become deeds. |
| GERTRUDE STEIN | I like anything that a word<br>can do—and the words do do<br>and they can do<br>what they never do do. |
| ROBERT FROST | Poetry is the renewal of words forever and ever. |

## THE SPIRIT OF PLAY

When we say that the principle most at work behind the language of poetry is the spirit of play—we must understand how the word "play" is used.

Play has a light external side as well as a serious internal side. On its light side, it means fun, amusement, tomfoolery. But on its serious side, "play" means more than mere fun or frolic—it means the quality of brisk movement.

We mean the quality of briskness, a quick nimble movement and activity (as in a play of swords)—where the essential thing meant is activity, as in a play of lights, a play of colors, a play of fountains.

From merely visual and physical activity, "play" can move on to the mental realm, as in a play of wits or a play of life and death. What is important now is the paradox—play of ideas—the contrast and contest of opposing forces.

So, from light musical-verbal play, we can move to intellectual and dramatic play—to paradox and wit, to irony and tragic play. In both senses, play engages the mind of the poet and therewith the language of poetry and the depth of poetry.

However, now a warning—One should not overplay. Cummings sometimes overplayed his fragmentation of words, producing only eccentricity. Stevens overplayed his language, producing nothing more than arabesques, doodles and hollow grill work.

• • •

Not until you have developed and cultivated your life together with your art can you utter and create the required language for poetry. The process of learning language and technique will take *at least* ten years of devoted study.[23]

---

23 This was not merely Villa's assessment. Cummings, in an essay entitled *A Poet's Advice to Students*, wrote of the difficulty of, as he put it, "expressing nobody-but-yourself in words" in these terms: "Nothing is quite as easy as using words like somebody else. We all of us do exactly this nearly all of the time—and whenever we do it, we're not poets. If, at the end of your first ten or fifteen years of fighting and working and feeling, you find you've written one line of one poem, you'll be very lucky indeed." From E. E. Cummings, *A Miscellany*, George J. Firmage, ed. (New York:The Argophile Press, 1958), 13.

## CHAPTER SEVENTEEN

# Introduction to Poetic Technique

We now begin our study of the *technique* of poetry, or of how a poem is written.

Although a poem arises from the unconscious (subconscious), it is however shaped up by the conscious mind—so you must learn to be a skilled worker. Technique is the *means*, not the goal, of art. Learning technique will be the main goal of the remainder of this book, because it is the only break-through to art.

We are moving from the *theory of poetry*, general poetics, to the *theory of the poem*, to technical poetics—concerned with the specific situation called the poem.

A poem differs from poetry in that, before the poem is complete, it is already poetry. But it is poetry only. When the work attains completeness, as a mechanism or construction, then it is a poem, not only poetry. It is both poetry and a poem.

St. John Perse, the French poet, said that he chose to be a poet "because poetry demands the maximum of responsibility in the fact of writing and the fact of life." Many amateurs consider the "fact of life" alone and are unaware of the "fact of writing."

The inexperienced writer is easily self-persuaded to take the power of his or her starting emotion as the measure of his or her writing. Consequently, he or she sees only what he or she intended to write. Such writers will not see the poverty of their own writing even if it is pointed out to them.

That is why, as artists, we need to learn to maintain an aesthetic distance from our work—a workable detachment from our feelings so that we can view our work with objectivity. Let us get involved in the technicalities of the medium to achieve the "fact of writing." Marianne Moore, for example, saw no reason to call her work poetry—"except that there is no other category in which to put it." Here we celebrate civilized writing—civilized beauty.

The artist does not express his or her feelings—what he or she expresses is the feeling of the work. The work decides its own feelings, disregards the artist's feelings. "Art is a statement by an outsider, from within." Hortense Calisher.

Self expression is discussed (denounced) in Chapter 2. The diamond is colorless, which is all colors. You must have the diamond (poem) clear (colorless) and *let* the colors come through. You cannot make it happen, you must *let* it happen. You have an obligation not to meddle with the work. You must maintain psychical or aesthetic distance.

Writing of poetry, as said before, is very difficult. Franz Kafka: "The path from the head to the pen is much longer and harder than from the head to the tongue." Words are the most difficult medium of all materials of art, because the poet must simultaneously express:

1. **visual beauty**—he works as a painter;
2. **beauty of sound**—he works as a musician;
3. **beauty of movement**—he works as a dancer;
4. **beauty of form**—he works as a sculptor;
5. **soundness of structure**—he works as an architect; and
6. at the same time make an **intellectual statement**—as a man of the mind.

All the arts are present in poetry (and vice versa). The poet must have musical craft, linguistic craft, the craft of versification, visual craft, rhythmic craft, logical craft, and the craft of intelligence.

All of the problems of poetry writing are technical. The work of Cummings sometimes looks very "free," but in fact he was one of the great technicians in poetry. In order to be a technician in poetry, one must confront art as a problem. Georges Bracque, the French painter: "All art starts as a problem, and ends with a prayer." André Gide: "Every work of art is a problem solved."

The artist is always looking for a problem to solve and this problem is always aesthetic. The artist creates the problem himself. He solves the problem as best he can—he finds technical solutions for the problems that he creates.

The poet resists the easiness of self expression. He or she creates resistances in his or her language. He or she deliberately places technical difficulties in his or her way. Everything is tentative and provisional until the correct language comes along. The poet presses language until what is said is good and right. He or she gets meaning from language after wrestling with it, and the language of poets is not explainable in prose terms. The poem is a revelation to the poet, who is surprised by what he or she has said. Thus poets learn by their poems; they do not teach their poems.

Formalism constructs the reality of the work. Where there is no technical solution, there is no reality constructed. Marshall McLuhan: "Problems become discoveries."

In nature, beauty is an accident but in art beauty is always deliberate and worked for. A beautiful poem is not an accident.

> ANDRÉ GIDE: Art is always the result of some constraint. To hold that [art] rises higher the freer it is, is to hold that what keeps the kite from climbing is the string to which it is attached.

Art thrives on limitations. A poem demands restrictions for its successful expression—and the poet, since there are no prescribed rules, creates his or her own with each poem that he or she writes.

Poetry, as a problem of art, is a problem of technique, and not a problem of thought or meaning. The poet imposes difficulties on his or her own work—sets checks and constraints—such as artificial rhythm, rhymes, pattern, suspensions—technical hazards that he or she has to outwit or iron out. The poet has to scour his or her resources in order to overcome these hurdles. He or she uses the medium not only as a vehicle but as an obstacle so that he or she is in a state of both mastery and helplessness. He or she wants the achievement to be as difficult as possible. The good poet turns limitations into assets.

Robert Frost asked Austin Clarke, an English poet, "What kind of verse do you write?" Clarke responded: "I load myself with chains and try to get out of them." There you have an image of a poet as like Houdini. The image is not fanciful at all, as every poet knows. All the fine poets are and have been Houdinis getting out of their chains. When working as a poet laden with chains, you still can appear to move effortlessly, and then you are an artist.

I find enjoyable in writing poems this process of making a problem for myself and, once it is created, find its very presence a pleasure as well as a challenge—then, its correct solution becomes a thrilling experience.

> JOHANN WOLFGANG VON GOETHE: A man is a poet if the difficulties inherent in his art provide him with ideas; he is not a poet if they deprive him of ideas.

> PAUL VALÈRY: [I]t is a pleasure which arouses the intelligence, defies it, and makes it love its defeat.

**Figure 7.** The following cartoon was presented by Villa as an illustration of the poet happily working with his constraints (resistances).

"*There's a happy Puritan.*"

**Figure 8.** The following depiction of Pegasus—described in Chapter 12 as the symbol of lyric poetry because of the poem's lyrical qualities that enable it to take off and fly high—on the back of a turtle, perhaps the slowest moving thing in creation, was presented by Villa to illustrate that the achievement of such heights is only accomplished by the slow and difficult process of identifying and overcoming technical obstacles to successful completion of the poem.

Why is the poetic process slow and difficult? Because, as John Hall Wheelock explained:

> The truth that is a poem must, like any wild thing, be stalked; it will never be taken alive by direct assault. Step by step,...the poet approaches. Stealthily, through endless circles of trial and error, revision and elimination, he saunters around the prey. Line by line and sentence by sentence, its form and contours grow clearer. The net of language is flung; coil by coil, loop by loop, it is tightened until, at long last, the poet is able to examine and to understand what it is he has, so long, so arduously, so deliriously, been pursuing. The thing he may find there will often astound him.

William Faulkner, comparing Thomas Wolfe with Ernest Hemingway:

> I rated the authors on the basis of their splendid failure to do the impossible. I believed Wolfe tried to do the greatest of the impossible.... I rated Hemingway last because he stayed within what he knew. He did it fine, but he didn't try for the impossible.

> JACQUES MARITAIN: No one is expected to do the impossible; that is what the poet is required to do.

"Thank God," said Dylan Thomas, "the writing is becoming daily more difficult."

> EDITH SITWELL: The poet accomplishes his design instinctively, but at the same time with knowledge. In him, knowledge has become instinct, and during the conception of the poem, knowledge works in him as if it were nature alone. When the work is almost completed, when the inspiration has pronounced its aim, then and only then, does the knowledge become conscious knowledge once again.

The 18th Century French philosopher, art critic and writer, Denis Diderot, wrote:

> In our day, men of genius have transferred philosophy from the intelligible world to the real world. Will there ever be a man to do the same for lyrical poetry, to bring it down from enchanted realms to the earth we inhabit?

In his play, *Him*, E. E. Cummings offered his perception of a good poet:

> Imagine a human being who balances three chairs, one on top of another, on a wire, eighty feet in the air with no net underneath, and then climbs into the top chair, and begins to swing....

There you have a depiction of poetry's tightrope esthetic mentioned in Chapter I.

We are now ready to concern ourselves with the *poem itself*, the formal object that is the result of the *poetic process* and its principles. We will learn how to make the poem "move in knowledge" and how to make the poem become itself—reach its true poetics.

Again, a *caveat*: Do not think when you read and absorb what this book will teach you, you will be poets. As said previously, it may take ten years or more to become a poet who is an artist, and no one can guarantee that you ever will. However, you will certainly have an appreciation of what a poem is as a serious art work and of what a poet is as artist. You will be enabled to assess the measure of the poem's success by coming to the medium and reading a poem technically, evaluating the lyrical spirit that drives the poem, as well as the language. You will also, at a glance, be able to cast aside free verse (in the sense discussed in Chapter 11) and other maladies of the untrained poet.

We will study the step-by-step details, the ploys and strategies, and the off-stage manipulations of a poem in the making. We will parse out in detail each step of the poem-making process. Where there is no technical excellence, there is no technical interest, and where there is no technical interest there is no work of art.

When Whistler painted a portrait of his mother, he entitled the work *Arrangement in Black and Gray*. His interest as an artist was not in his mother, but in the formal factors, in the formal arrangement of the work. As we rise in aesthetic cultivation, we develop an objective detachment from subject matter, and pay our respectful concern especially to form.

As we study technique, we will see how true Valèry's words are that "the process of making a poem is far more interesting than the work itself." (*Aesthetics*, 137). Georges Bracque: "It is *not* the ultimate goal which is interesting, but the *means* by which we arrive there." It is lack of knowledge of this means that prevents many would-be poets from becoming poets.

Technique is not easy. It requires patience and gradual learning. At the end of one's life, an artist realizes that he or she is still learning how to improve his or her art. Jean Cocteau said: "One has to enter into art as one goes into a monastic order."

### THE ADJECTIVES FOR POETRY

So far there is only one adjective for poetry—"poetic." However, "poetic" is a very *un*specialized word—it is not limited to poetry but can refer to prose as well, as well as a host of other things: "poetic novel," "poetic piece of music," "a poetic fantasy," "a poetic landscape," "poetic justice," etc. The import of "poetic" is quintessential and refers mainly to essence and spirit.

I propose two new terms: Let us use the adjective "poetric" when referring to the discipline, the technical efficacy in the use of the artistic medium of verse. Thus, Marianne Moore's poems are poetric, although they are not poetic. Dylan Thomas and Cummings are both poetric and poetic. All "poets" who lack the technical discipline of verse are non-poetric.

The other new adjective that I propose is "poeimic"—which should refer to the special and particular requirements of the lyric poem. These are: 1) the necessity of a dynamic first line, 2) that the language carry music, 3) an inner dramaturgy—a thematic rise and development to climax; and 4) brevity or economy.

By this poeimic standard, Wallace Stevens' "Sea Surface Full of Clouds," in *Twentieth Century American Poetry* (111), and Marianne Moore's poems are not poeimic, mainly because they have no dramaturgy, no dramatic development and gathering up into sense, although they are poetric, i.e., they satisfy the requirements of fine versification.

However, Cummings, Eberhart, Hopkins, Donne, and Emily Dickinson are all poeimic, besides being poetric and poetic. Coleridge's "The Ancient Mariner" is not poeimic because, although it has dramaturgy, it is a narrative and is extended, thus missing the qualities of beauty and brevity. Poetric is stricter in degree than poetic, and poeimic is stricter than poetric.

In the study of the technique of poetry, we are not so much dealing with poetic but poetric (which refers to verse structure) and with poeimic (which refers to the more specific demands of lyric poetry).

## RETURNING TO TECHNIQUE

Technique can be measured—if you have been trained and cultivated to see its value. Technique is the proof of art. The poet, in writing a poem, is on the line to prove his or her prowess with language and form—is organizing a game between language and form. Technique is the organizing capacity of the poet; it is managerial and therefore he or she must develop maneuvers and strategies (as in the game of chess).

High technique is where you cash in on every possible move, on every possible position and modulation—on every possible precision—so that the action on the medium is at the richest and fullest and has authority.

High technique attacks the medium on all sides and from every angle. After you get used to its riches, you can no longer be satisfied with less.

Technique can be classified in any one of three conditions:

1. *Low Technique*: or elementary technique—that is what you find in Blake, Keats, Shelley, Wordsworth, Browning and Tennyson. It is simplistic technique, without subtleties or modulations.
2. *Medium Technique*: the intermediate grade—Wallace Stevens and Dylan Thomas—it is more developed but deficient in highlights.
3. *High Technique*: full of highlights, immediacies, full of action at every point—Hopkins, Cummings, M. Moore.

Cummings is the Elvis Presley of poetry—he gyrates poetry like a pelvis, full of thrusts and grinds.

Art grows by technique—art always develops and grows by refinement of technique.

## CHAPTER EIGHTEEN

# The Inception of the Poem

Stéphane Mallarmé described the terror and sense of sterility the poet experiences when he sits down to write a poem and confronts the blank sheet of paper and no words come to him. His suggestion was that the poet, after an interval of time, simply get up from his chair and produce the blank sheet of paper as the poem he sat down to write. Could one imagine anything that is more expressive of the poet's feelings of inner devastation than the virginal paper?[24]

And so we turn to the topic of just how does the poet start a poem. Is it *inspiration*? Jean Cocteau: "It is *not* inspiration—it is *ex*piration—it's getting it out of you." He also said that: "Poetry comes from elsewhere, an uninvited guest."

A poem begins in *silence*, at a moment of *poetic intuition*—at this point it is nothing but a *stir* or *fervor*. The best way is not to wait for such metaphorical twitches.

> JULES RENARD, *the French writer:* "A poet inspired—is a poet who writes faulty verse."
>
> "I am trying to work; thing is to light a little lamp in the brain. After that, it burns by itself."

Some suggested ways of starting the poem:

1. The easiest way is to have good luck—to have a good line—a germinal given phrase, a spontaneous formation, complete or incomplete, a "drop from Heaven" or from the ceiling or rising out of nowhere—it simply springs up. Howard Nemerov: "This is a mystery, at least in the sense that I cannot explain it—why should a phrase come to you out of the ground and seem to be exactly right?" It may not be a whole line—it may not

24 In his *selected poems and new* (New York: McDowell, Obolensky, 1958), 133, Villa took the first step beyond the above-suggested course of action, entitling a blank sheet of paper: "The Emperor's New Sonnet."

even be a phrase—it may only be a word or a couple of words. But such words when "dropped from Heaven," have such an energy in them that other words come clustering around them.

2. Sometimes a poet's mind begins to twitch because there is "an uncomfortable secret at the edge of his consciousness."

   JOHN HALL WHEELOCK: Writers have noted the feeling of discomfort experienced by the writer who carries within himself a work not yet written and which, even before it has been undertaken, 'wants to come out.'

   ETIENNE GILSON: A nudge in the mind is soon accompanied by an upsurge in energy, an almost physical provocation to do something and so he starts writing.

   ALBERT EINSTEIN: You can't scratch if you don't itch.

   The itch causes the poet to express. Some people call it a "feeling" but philosophers know it is not an emotion, but simply an itch.

3. The "cuss method"—P.J. Wodehouse suggested that you "sit at your desk and cuss a bit and something will come to you." You will be surprised—it works—and therefore is a recommended method.

4. The single word method: take any word and play around with it—you will come up with a combination of words that can start a poem.[25]

5. The ready-made method—fortuitous in that it is produced by chance or accident. If one has a good poetic eye, he may find ready-made lines for poetry in newspapers or magazines or online, and these are like free pollen to fertilize your imagination. One may even take a word or phrase from a good poem and go from there. T.S. Eliot, in a 1920 essay on the Elizabethan dramatist, Philip Massinger: "Immature poets imitate; mature poets steal..."

---

25 Villa, in his *selected poems and new*, 29, has a poem that begins: "Be beautiful, noble, like the antique ant." He explained that the poem began with the word "antique," which "was not enough because lacking in rhythm"; next came "ant," which was still lacking in rhythm and needed something before or after, thus leading to the first line from which the poem was propelled.

I would say that the most usual way with poets in starting a poem is the second method, which starts with song—the musical stir of song—and then descends into speech rather than ascending from speech. Therefore I will amplify on the characteristics of that method.

> JACQUES MARITAIN: The essential emotion is not an emotion to be expressed—but an emotion that causes to express."

Let us call it the "itch and twitch" method. What is the nature of this itch? Usually it is a buzz in the poet's mind—an abstract rhythm, abstract but palpable and can be felt, without words and without thought, a *bare percussion*. It is something singing abstractly in the head and asserting itself. It is poetic intuition that wants to transform itself into *verbal sound.*

> T.S. ELIOT: "I know that a poem...may tend to realize itself first as a particular rhythm before it reaches expression in words, and that this rhythm may bring to birth the idea and the image."

(It should be clear that idea, which is prose-fathering, is not poem-fathering, which is the province of language and music.)

Poetic intuition—the poet's subconscious has been fertilized by music—into words.

In his *Aesthetics*, Paul Valéry gave testimony in what is a detailed description of the second method:

> One day I was obsessed by a rhythm which suddenly became quite palpable in my mind.... The rhythm asserted itself with a certain authority. I had the feeling that it wanted to be embodied, to attain the perfection of being. But the only way in which it could become clearer in my consciousness was to borrow...elements of speech, syllables, words; and at this stage in this formation, the syllables and words were determined no doubt by their musical values and affinities...Rhythmic quality was the sole determinant of what should enter into the poem... This was the second step, the first having been the naked rhythm, the percussion pure and simple. Then, by a sort of awakening of the consciousness...substitutions occurred in the syllables, words were provisionally summoned up, and a definite line made its appearance...But this line in turn demanded a musical and logical continuation. The machine had been set going. (130)

Having discovered his or her first line, the poet then grows the poem on paper.[26] And the poem, once written, lives best on paper. In fact, the poet's immortality depends on paper—no paper, no immortality.

A poet cannot complete a poem solely in his or her head—he or she must see it on paper—actually see the form so that he or she can control and manipulate it. Unless visible to the eye, form is unimaginable—either that or it is completely lost, as happens when poems are read aloud. No idea of form can pass through the ears—only the musicality of the poem is thus conveyed.

The poem shapes better and forms better on paper because you can see it—thus finality of form can be grasped only from paper, not from sounds loose in the air. The visibility of poetry is important and the musicality of poetry is important—but reading it aloud is not at all important. Paper is the poet's battlefield where he will conquer or suffer defeat.

**Figure 9.** The poet's dilemma when he begins a poem prompted Villa to include the following Stallworthy poem in his lecture materials.

SCRIBO ERGO SUM

The page stares through me, like a mirror
With nothing in its eye
But ceiling or blank sky

No trick of the light, no paper error
Defines this emptiness.
Now I am featureless,

Unselved, without substance or image--
Till pen stroke by pen stroke
Out of the stubborn block

Of the page, forehead and mouth emerge,
Mouth moving and moving arm,
I write, therefore I am.

-- Jon Stallworthy

---

26 In this day and age of word processors, Villa might have added: "or on any of the digital media."

> PAUL VALÉRY: We communicate in black and white, with which nature can do nothing. She can do nothing with a bit of ink. She needs...infinite material, whereas we [poets] virtually need none, but, if possible, a great deal of intelligence...for the greater glory of black and white.

The poet's problem is indeed quite absurd. He or she is beginning a poem: 1) without language, especially when he or she starts from a musical stir in his or her mind, 2) without a form and 3) without an idea. The problem is therefore enormous—to find a form for a thought. The poetic intuition that begins a poem only activates, but does not know the form your poem is going to take or the thought that it will finally convey. However, unless you have a body (form) for the poem there cannot be a thought contained.

By body is meant not any amorphous, sprawling mass of words as in free verse or self expression, but a body that is shapely, that has contours and movement that has been erected and shaped by technical control and manipulation.

In finding the thought, "to catch the meaning out of the air / yet have it inviolably there" (R. Eberhart—"Hardening into Print"), you will find it "inviolably there" in the poetizing act only through the help of technique.

### PROBLEM OF THE FIRST LINE

A first line is needed—without it, there would be nothing to push forward that could grow into a poem. A first line need not be a complete statement—it can be only a phrase that is later enlarged.

You should not be worried if your first line does not mean anything. Let the first line mean what it may. You are working on the principle of discovery. You will, therefore, if you are a poet, discover your meaning as the poem goes along.

But you should worry if your first line is absurd or nonsensical. It does not matter if the first line has no meaning provided it is not absurd. We say the "first line" but we may mean opening lines—because the first line "given" to us may have to be broken into more than one line. Therefore the term "first line" may mean the overall line.

The poet John Ciardi: "A poem is a tail tucking a cat on top of itself." This tells how the poem is built—first, a tail, your first line, and then on top of your tail a "cat." That is how the cat looks structurally when you look at a sitting cat—its body mounted on its tail—although (since the poem is written downward on the page) the picture of the cat reverses—the cat is standing on its head with its tail raised above it. This depiction is accurate because the poem (the cat) does not find its head, its brains, its point, until the end of the poem.

Because we start working on the first line, we should make a close scrutiny of it—is it serviceable or not?—is it worth going forward with it or not? If you determine that your first line is not worth seeing, let it go. We should always work consciously, especially as we are working with an art. We should work to consciously design that art.

## Qualities That a Good First Line Should Have

A first line should be attention-catching and have immediate impact. If possible, it should be like an anvil blow—so that it attracts, teases, and entices at once. It must strike fast, have immediate strength or impact and be as startling and provocative as a newspaper headline. It should deliver the same kind of blow for the reader as for the poet. With the first line, the poem should catch fire and be in instant orbit.

A good first line must have momentum, the ability to take off and zoom. Without the latter quality, there will be no propulsion, no future activity, in the line. The principle of the poem's growth is hidden and embedded in the first line, and it is made up primarily of language and sound—verbal music—that is going to determine the growth of the poem into a complete poem.

However, your first line may be a false start. It may not be functional at all as a first line; it may lack the proper "rightness" with which to begin a poem. A great deal of reading and constant practice is necessary to discern what is required.

The first line, if not "right," may be a better fit for the body of the poem. It may even be a better fit for a last line. (Keep in mind, however, that if you work from a last line, you will be employing a prose process in poetry, where you work backward with the last line providing meaning that has not been discovered through the poetic process.)

One might almost say a poet who did not recognize a good first line could never write a good poem. A good first line must have momentum and be instantly flammable. Good first lines not only conquer your interest but make your mind salivate. For instance, "Deliver us *to* evil" (not "from").

A good first line is always compact. It has a terseness of condensation, because of the lyric demand for economy. With T.S. Eliot's poem "*The Waste Land*," Ezra Pound persuaded Eliot to excise the first fifty-four lines of the poem as Eliot had initially written it.

The strength of a first line can come in several ways:

1. By strength of language
   a. as metaphor: D. Thomas: "Altarwise by owl-light in the half-way house" and "A process in the weather of the heart"; E. Dickinson: "The suburbs of a secret" and "The Face we choose to miss."
   b. as aphorism—E. Dickinson: "Tell the truth but tell it slant" and "The soul should always stand ajar."

2. By music
   a. as word play—G.M. Hopkins: "How to keep—is there any any, nowhere / known some, bow or brooch or braid or brace, láce, latch / or catch or key to keep / Back beauty, keep it, beauty, beauty, beauty, ...from vanishing away?"
   b. by strength of music—D. Thomas: "Especially when the October wind / With frosty fingers punishes my hair"; Cummings: "All in green went my love riding / on a great horse of gold."

3. Strength of dramatic tension—E. Dickinson: "I cannot live with you, / It would be life"; G.M. Hopkins: "Not, I'll not, carrion comfort, despair, not feast on thee."

4. Strength of image—John Denwood: "When in a mirror of a permanent tear."

5. Strength of incidental idea:
   a. concept: W.S. Merwin: "No need to break the mirror / Here is the face shattered"; E. Dickinson: "Meeting by accident / we hovered by design" and "Because I could not stop for Death, / He kindly stopped for me"; Cummings: "the Cambridge ladies who live in furnished souls."
   b. paradox: E. Dickinson: "I cannot live with you , / It would be life" and "Your riches taught me poverty."
   c. cryptic/mystery: E. Dickinson: "Morning that comes but once / Considers coming twice" and "A little madness in the Spring / Is wholesome even for the King."

6. Strength from magic or charm: E. Dickinson: "How soft a caterpillar steps" and "Perhaps you'd like to buy a flower? / But I could never sell."

7. Originality—E. Dickinson: "This is my letter to the world, / That never wrote to me."

Paul Valéry described the development of a "consequent" or "continuant" first line in his *Aesthetics*:

> In another case, a line came to me, obviously engendered by its sound, its timbre. The meaning suggested by the unexpected element of a poem, the image it evokes, the syntactical figure it presented (an opposition) acted like a little crystal in a supersaturated solution and led me as though by symmetry to expect and to construct...a beginning before my line, to prepare the way for it and justify its existence, and after it a continuation to round out its effect. Thus, from a single line there developed, little by little, all the elements of a poem...(130)

All art consists of doing until you have accomplished the deed. "Do" is a very important word in art. Just as important is the word "don't." One should know the *don'ts* of the art he or she practices as well as what should be done.

### THE "DON'TS" OF THE ART OF POETRY

The principal *don'ts*—which apply to the body of the poem as well as to the first line—are:

- If you can say it in prose, don't write it as poetry.
- Don't state or declare—don't be declarative or make direct statements. Poetry is art off-center—it is oblique and avoids being explicit. Poetry is a language of indirection, not of directness. By direct statement, only the meaning is emphasized. The language itself, its feeling, sensuality and tone, are not conveyed and experienced. The method of indirection enables these elements to come to the fore and thus the line is enabled to attain more verbal surface as well as more verbal depth and tension. This is what is meant by the statement that poetry evokes. Indirection is concealment...and yet is revelation. The poet conceals and—at the same time—reveals. However, if your line states (sometimes it is unavoidable), it must be statement plus. The "plus" is important—you must declare only with power or mystery.

- Don't describe—description impedes the poetic velocity, which resides in the metaphor, and will turn the lightning swiftness of poetry into the dragging pace of prose.
- Don't be literal and obvious. To be literal is to express only the obvious and apparent sense and take things at face value. Where language is merely literal or factual, overtly expressing an idea, there is no expressiveness and the result is flatness and the effect of prose. The antonym to literal is metaphysical. To move by the energy of metaphor is the modality for poetry. The metaphor works by largesse—by enlargement—it entitles the line not just to one flat meaning but to all of its potentials. A poem should have a dimension of meaning beyond mere meaning. Linguistic language, the language of poetry (the Art of Speech), is not literal.
- Don't be naïve.
- Don't use the past tense, which is the prose tense. This gives a work a narrative effect, as if you were telling a story. The past tense is mainly for fiction.
- Avoid any time chronology, which also gives a work a narrative effect.
- Don't use clichés—trite expressions that are grubby and suffering from mildew—words and phrases so overused that they are meaningless and no longer have any effect. Instead of creating a positive effect, they create a negative effect, against the poem and the poet. The cultivated and educated reader realizes that this is fossil language, moth-eaten and fly-specked. A literate reader is suffocated and stops reading.
- Don't use words that you do not understand.
- Don't overuse adjectives—avoid adjectival embroidery—in fact, avoid all adjectives when possible. Don't "dress up" language. Dressy language is messy language and needs to be cleaned. For poetry, which needs essence uppermost, adjectives are delimiting and weakening and remain just décor.
- Don't use compound words.

- Don't make enumerations—only Walt Whitman was entitled to do that.
- Don't use overkill language—gaudy and bloated language. Don't inflate—avoid big, pompous words. Don't show off by torturing language—it merely destroys the clarity and cleanliness that should be there. It is best for you now (as you are developing as a poet) to acknowledge the beauty of simplicity and not be afraid of it. Where you intend your poem to be serious, bloated language can produce a comic effect. Cocteau once remarked that among the arts of life is knowing "just how far to go too far."
- Don't overplay language—as if poetry were a finger exercise. Although poetry involves the spirit of play, poetry should not do the boogie-woogie. There is a proper amount for everything. Finger exercises only get tedious; they are trivial.
- Don't bleed and be sentimental—don't emotionalize yourself into the poem, but let the poem grow of its own feeling, if it can.
- Don't be clever—so clever, so chic, so crappy.
- Don't be vulgar.
- Don't be nonsensical.
- Don't make sick statements—avoid absurd, preposterous ideas and images.
- Don't be lengthy—a lyric poem is like a sketch which, although it is not filled out with details, is still filled in with essentials. Lengthiness is looseness in poetry. Be concise—poetry not only is brief—it is compacted—deliberately made so.
- Don't glue phrases together.
- Don't be in love with yourself or your work, especially with your early poems. The best thing to do may be simply to forget them.

• • •

In general, the poet takes a close-up view of words and savors them as a jeweler does gems—for their brilliance, their weight, their individuality, their lights and their shadows. The poet sees words from the outside in and from the inside out. He writes from the inside and outside of words, but he writes from the outside first.

Wallace Stevens: "Words...are the eye grown larger, more intense."

The poet uses the word *for itself*, for its own sensory sake, he uses it *positively* as word—for joy in the word *as word.*

All in all, from the very first line, the poet must be indirect and economic; these are the two great virtues of poetry. The indirect way is not the roundabout and therefore the lengthier way, the uneconomic way, but the way to suggest and evoke. Poetry is carried language—it reaches its destination by the leap and curve of the imagination.[27]

---

27 Villa reported that in every year in which he was writing poetry, he re-read the complete works of Dylan Thomas, Eleanor Wylie, John Donne, Walt Whitman, Cummings, Gerard Manley Hopkins and Emily Dickinson.

## CHAPTER NINETEEN

# Propulsion of the First Line into a Poem

The first line is still only a seed, an embryo—the poet still has to face the problem of growing this seed, to build on it, to create a substructure with dimension and form and completeness. And, of course, the work is not easy.

The poet's ability to complete the poem is his or her true test as an artist.

In the propulsion and development of the poem, the first line should give off intimations of what the next lines should be. The first line has a capacity for steering and directing—it is predictive and anticipates, it envisions and generates what follows.

In good poetry, what the poem is going to be is predestined by the qualities of the first line. The predestination is, to begin with, verbal and textural, dependent mainly upon the sensory organic aspects of the first line.

The first line is a dynamic field—an arsenal and repository of forces that forecast and presage what the poem is going to be.

By its textural and verbal properties, by its qualities as material and fabric, the first line will induce the further language, the next lines.

In poetry, if you are a good poet, the language arising in your head and that you have not written down yet will obey the direction of the lines of force in the first line. They will fall in shape in the way that iron filings thrown on a magnetic field will follow the directions set by the lines of force of the magnet. These lines of force will magnetize out of your head the concrete music, the concrete language and the concrete sense of the poem you are writing.

What are these lines of force?

1. A *musical* line of force—which is a kernel of rhythm, with its own direction and energy. This line of force creates a *musical situation*—which must be fulfilled by succeeding lines.

2. A *verbal* line of force—a kernel of verbal texture, of words as sensory and physical objects with their own direction and energy. The *verbal* line of force creates for the poem a *verbal, textural situation*, which exploits the linguistic textural properties of the first line and which must be fulfilled along the same lines so that they all are of one cloth.

3. There is a *tiny semantic* line of force—a tiny beginning for thought or meaning.

The set of words in the first line is still unorganized as meaning and with incomplete relations. However, some glimmer of meaning, although confused and unrealized, is already engaged. This tenuous meaning, still vague and hazy—unlike the *musical* and *verbal* lines of force which are strong and must pursue their own specific directions—can go in any direction. The *semantic* line of force has no direction because you don't know your meaning yet.

The *musical* line of force and *verbal* line of force must materialize as language in order to be poetry.

Instead of the poet imposing his or her feelings on the poem—it is the poem that makes the poet feel and finally say something. The poem he or she is writing causes the poet to feel, to have feelings, and to have something to say. The poem is the cause for feeling and thought rather than the effect (result) of feeling and thought.

By his or her ability to discern lines of force in his or her material, by proper nurturing of these through intelligence and technique, the poet achieves a poem. It is the material that teaches the artist.

These three lines of force must work in complicity so that they grow in a line, in harmony, in unison, for they have a corporate purpose. Only versification can harness these forces of poetry and structure them into form.

**Figure 10.** The following diagram depicts these three lines of force and how they work in complicity with one another.

| | | | | |
|---|---|---|---|---|
| M. L/F (rhythm) | Strong<br>-------→ | 1 direction | : | Musical Situation |
| V. L/F (language) | S<br>-------→ | 1 direction | : | Verbal Situation |
| S. L/F (meaning) | Weak<br>^<br>< ----I---- ><br>v | no/all/any | : | Semantic Situation |

After the first line:

| | | | |
|---|---|---|---|
| **Technical Force (Technique)** | **Strong**<br>^<br>< ----I---- ><br>v | : | **Versic Situation** |

The strong musical and verbal lines of force and the weak semantic line of force spring from the qualities of the poem's first line. The musical and verbal lines of force arise from the carnal energies of poetry, whereas the semantic line of force arises from the intellectual and spiritual energies of the first line. The technical force (technique) has nothing to do with the qualities of the first line, but is the product of the work of the poet himself.

Many would-be poets do not see these lines of force in the first line and cannot complete the poem. When you can perceive the invisible lines of force and carry them forward throughout the poem, you are a poet.

After the first line, all the rest is calculated verse. The proper meaning of "versification" is calculated verse. Technique means the use of calculated verse. Precision, Order and Elegance are the qualities of technique.

The technical force (technique) can go in any direction depending upon the way the first line is versified. Take, for example, a first line: "The sun keeps its riddles." It may be written in one line or two, but the second line may take two forms:

The sun
      keeps its riddles

or

The sun keeps
its riddles

Each of these methods of versifying the first line will result in different versification of the following lines and different stanza patterns.

The good poet produces self-defending poems, poems that defend themselves against time by virtue of their craft. You cannot chip away at such poems, for they have engineered their own defense. They exist as works of art but their form has created a battlement against time.

Please study Marianne Moore's "The Fish" for it is a poem of absolute technical mastery—where versification has created facets as on a diamond, so that the structure of the poem has refractions and reflections like a crystal.

> PAUL VALÉRY: It is not the accomplished work that can fulfill and edify us, but only the way in which we have done it. Art and its difficulties increase our stature.

As the poem proceeds beyond the first line, a new situation arises—a technical situation, as verse and structure, which we will call the *versic situation*.[28] This *versic situation* will control:

- the line lengths and the line movement; which in turn will determine
- the stanza pattern; which in turn governs
- stanzaic movement; and eventually
- the poem's total form.

And, the *versic situation* will also give logical direction to the emerging meaning—unearth, select and utilize the most advantageous semantic thread (or line of meaning) in accordance with the movement and versic necessities of the poem. Again, this technical and versic force springs from the poet's own force—not from the qualities of the first line.

The versic force in a good poet should be as strong as the musical and verbal forces. If the versic force is not strong, the musical and verbal forces go to waste, because technical incompetence nullifies everything in art. It is the versic force that leads and guides the poem—that is why the study of technique is essential to becoming a good poet.[29]

---

28 Villa coined the term "versic" as adjectival shorthand for versification and, with this understanding, that usage will be followed herein.

29 Villa explained that the versic force is the only force he could teach. He noted that Marianne Moore and Richard Wilbur were not profound poets but very good craftsmen, so they should be looked to in developing technical force.

We will now, in the succeeding chapters, separate these forces for analysis purposes, keeping in mind that they occur and work conjointly—in the poem they have one simultaneous corporate existence.

## CHAPTER TWENTY

# The Musical Situation

The musical situation springs from the musical line of force (or the rhythm), which is the executive of poetry: It is the main director of the verbal and semantic forces. It will cause the right language to step forward, to appear and materialize as the verbal language that is the flesh of poetry—and that will carry within its language the meaning of the poem.

> WALLACE STEVENS: Poetry "makes music seem to be a nature, a place in which itself—gives rise to everything else."

> DYLAN THOMAS: One disagrees with a line of poetry because one discovers, immediately or after re-reading, that it is not inevitable, it could be changed, the wrong words have been used, or the right words in the wrong order, indeed one changes them about in the mind as one reads; but when the inevitable line appears, what is there to say? The music is made; the magic is done; the sound and the spell remain.

> ROBERT FROST: I hear everything I write. All poetry is to me first a matter of sound.

You must see poetry first with your ears, for melody and musical rightness. Secondly, only with your eyes, for pattern and visual balances.

The musical line of force precedes the formation of new language and the words that come simply "fall in" with the rhythm. When a word comes, the poet listens to its sounds and must judge whether it can fall in line harmoniously with the musical line of force. If it cannot, it must be rejected.

> GEORGE STEINER: Music is, with mathematics, the principal language of the mind, when the mind is in a condition of non-verbal feeling.

In other words, the pure mind is either musical or mathematical or both.

The poet must compose always in the sequence of the musical phrase. That is the main principle of poetry. Poetry goes by the rhythm method.

As said before, the art of speech is not just speech but language plus. The first plus is music. It is the first imaginative increment in the art of poetry.

Poetry is sounds—that sound better because the sounds have been organized into music. Poetry is more the sound of thought than the thought itself, for poetry is built around a musical axis and not on a semantic axis. Therefore, music mandates the line.

> GEORGE STEINER: The interpenetration of poetry and music is so close that their origin is indivisible... The fortunes of Orpheus...are almost synonymous with the nature and functions of poetry.

The ear always patrols the line of poetry and the poet is always under standing orders to maintain the music. In poetry, words live only so long as their music lives. In poetry, the man who cannot sing: dies.

Poetry is tympanic—the ear acts as compass to tell you whether you are going in the right poetic direction. If the sounds are wrong, you are proceeding in the wrong direction.

Music is not interested in making meaning—it is interested in moving forward beautifully, that is all. Robert Frost: "If the sound is right, the sense will take care of itself."

> WILLIAM GASS ON PAUL VALÉRY (in the Bollingen edition of *The Collected Works of Paul Valéry*): How elusive the line is, wound in music like a gift in tissue, both wrapped and wrapping fragile as a bibelot...[30]

A poem is in essence a verbal concerto, a musical affair. A poem differs from a stage or movie "musical" in that it is not a musical version of something else. A poem is musical *per se*, from its very origin and beginning, because it is conceived from the first as musical sound.

The notes in music are only a musical score and still require rendition, but the language of a poem is both verbal score as well as its musical rendition.

Music, in lyric poetry, is not only obligatory and indispensable—it is its first major requirement. The poet's burden (and delight) is always to carry music.

Poetry is music verbalized, not speech musicalized. The language comes only to suit the music. The music comes first.

30 A bibelot is a small object whose value lies in its beauty or rarity.

**Figure 11.** Villa used R. P. Blackmur's poem, MISSA VOCIS, to illustrate how the musical force leads to the verbal force that produces the language to verbalize the music. The handwritten comments seen below are those of Villa.

MISSA VOCIS

Priest-mannerly the mind,
that president mask,
gives dogsight to the new blind,
priest-mannerly unknowing
what mastering ear-task
Musical Force keeps the great churn going.

O unmannerable heart, } Don't let your
monk-dancer, be still, } feeling rule your poem
be leashless, apart:
M. F. the sounding, the growing
unabettable will
sets the great churn going.

Lie chidden, lie dark,
in the reserved deep
lie prone, lie stark: } Subconscious Poetic Process
the unprayable flowing,
the vast sluiceage of sleep,
sets the great churn going.

In the wringing of new sound, } Poetic Pr-
chance flowering to choice,
Verbal Force old words in full round
in-breathing, thrall-throwing;
the mass of new voice New words based on
keeps the great churn going. previous letters + sounds

— R.P. Blackmur

Stéphane Mallarmé defined poetry as "*perfect music,* accompanied by the *idea.*" This definition is, however, faulty. Idea is not a companion of music; in poetry they are inseparable. The words of poetry not only dance the music and meaning, the music has also become the meaning, as the meaning has become music also.

In employing words musically, the poet is now using words non-lingually and he may be violating sense, but although such usages may seem "wrong," yet they are right, speaking in terms of artistic rightness.

It is not enough just to have sounds—prose has sounds. In poetry, the sounds must be woven into music.

A poet must know the refined luxuries of sound. He must weigh, taste and test each letter and syllable, word and phrase. He must have an auditory imagination as distinct from the visual imagination. Ned Rorem, for example, says that: "The word gold has six sounds...: guh-ah-oh-oo-ll-d."

> ROBERT FROST: The ear is the only true writer and the only true reader... To judge a poem...you...apply the one test—greatest test. You listen for the...sounds.

> EDITH SITWELL: With regard to the relationship of consonants and vowels, it might perhaps be said that the vowels are the spirit, the consonants... the physical reality, the garments of the vowel.

> LOUIS ZUKOFSKY: The vowels abide in consonants, like souls in bodies.

> RICHARD EBERHART: "The delirium of joy" inheres between "vowels, where lies the ultimate mystery of language" and "the rigidities of consonants."

> This whole interplay is an exercise in music.

Reading poetry is from the *eye*—to the *ear*—to the *brain*, and back to the *ear* again.

> ARCHIBALD MACLEISH: "The one poetic gift which no amount of application can purchase and which no amount of ingenuity can fake [is] a delicate and perceptive ear."

If your first line is not musical, the first and most proper thing to do is to discard it or upgrade it to musicality.

The poet, then, must have an *inner ear*—it is the ear that decides the rightness of things, the rightness of language, the rightness of tone, the rightness of movement, the rightness of versification and, ultimately, the rightness of sense.

The music of poetry is actually *not* music because it does not sing. As Auden said: "One can't be influenced as a poet by a composer because... [poetry and music] are two different arts."

As the poet, critic, and biographer of Robert Frost, Stanley Burnshaw, observed: "Poetry is written down for the *eye* to hear"—*not* the ear—but the "*eye* to hear."

To propel the first line forward, the poet should have the ability to hear the rhythm as abstract sound because it is abstract music after all—as abstract rhythm devoid of words, although waiting for words. John Dryden described this rhythm as "inarticulate poetry"—inarticulate because it has no words yet to give it concrete sounds. The rhythm is only mental or visual, not yet physical and so cannot be heard by the physical ear.

A good poet knows where his or her musical bar begins and ends, and pauses there, before he or she runs on again.

The net of projected abstract rhythm, the "inarticulate poetry," will make a catch of words that will fit in with the rhythm. The abstract rhythm transforms itself into verbal music, becomes converted into concrete words that carry out the abstract rhythm—but it is now concrete rhythm. Whatever idea enters the poem must hang on the words admitted by the rhythm of the first line and that is why it is the rhythm that must be projected—and if it cannot hang on this rhythm then the idea must give way to another that falls in line with the rhythm.

**Figure 12.** What was present in the first line as a musical line of force was an undercurrent—until with the musical growth of the lines you have also, simultaneously, made it into a concrete verbal current of words.

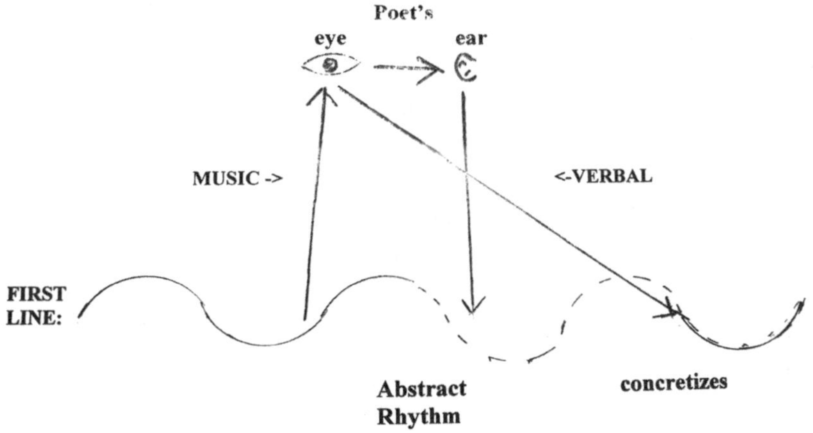


The musical and verbal currents in a poem concretize and materialize concurrently, at the same moment—and fuse and become one current. It is the main current of poetry—that of verbal music. Above is a visual depiction of the process whereby the poet fuses the musical and verbal currents of the first line to produce verbal music.

No words that do not fit in with the abstract rhythm are acceptable.

The semantic line of force will remain a subcurrent until nearly the end of the poem. It is only at the end of the poem that it will turn on its full force and concretize very suddenly.

The rhythms of verse are unnatural because the poet, as an artist, imposes arbitrary rhythms over the logical, natural rhythms found in prose and in ordinary speech. These unnatural rhythms are calculated and composed—consciously designed to create technical as well as musical and semantic tension. The pauses of verse are not the natural pauses of prose (which are the pauses of grammar and logic) but are versic, artistic pauses—the pauses of technique and art.

Pauses in poetry are more than rests in movement—in poetry a pause is "useful dead time"—not mere inactivity—so that the time is not dead at all. It is rhythm at counterpoint with the stress on the counterpoint—in order to give rhythm tension and thrust. The fine poet uses this counterpoint to create the pull of art versus the pull of natural speech. Otherwise you are merely talking.

The poetic pause achieved by arbitrary rhythm is contrapuntal—although it is a pause, it is actually a half-step move at the right moment, so that instead of halting the movement it vitalizes it.

In arbitrary rhythm there is this dislocation of natural rhythm for the purpose of artistic stress: by deranging the natural rhythm it gathers irregular accents to throw the inherent rhythm into relief and thus provides contrast as well as surprise—equivalent in effect to the artistic distortion found in the visual arts.

It is more difficult to break the line unnaturally. To break the line unnaturally with half-moves to inflect and brace up the line and still keep it in movement—that is where the art comes from.

For example, the first two lines in "*Canaan*" by Muriel Spark are: "She is committed to the earth and the earth / is plighted forever to her," whereas the natural rhythm is: "She is committed to the earth / and the earth is plighted forever to her."

> PAUL VALÉRY: If your rule is disorder / You will pay dearly / For having put things in order.

As verse, this would be written, however, as follows:

    If your rule is
disorder
    You will pay

    Dearly for having
put things
    in order.

## CHAPTER TWENTY-ONE

# The Verbal Situation

A good poem is a successful experiment in the pleasures of language and we will now see how to obtain or create those pleasures.

Poetry means verbal action—action by language—because poetry is an encounter in language.

It is in language that the poet proves and exhibits his or her creativity—as it is by the sense of form, by versification, that the poet proves his or her artistry.

Although the musical element of poetry is very strong and has captaincy—it however merely pilots the language; the poetic imagination displays itself not as music but as language. Language is the organic fact, the concrete manifestation of poetry; it is the central agency that holds music, tension and meaning together.

The language of poetry, although it is musical, is not music, but verbality. The abstract rhythm must be processed into a positive state—into material language of sensory qualities. Music is the source power of poetry—but what it targets is language.

The poet mentally experiments and tests further words to see whether such words can fulfill the rhythm as well as tally with the logical sense of his or her previous words.

> GERTRUDE STEIN: One of the things that is a very interesting thing to know—is how you are feeling inside you—to the words that are coming to be outside of you.

> DYLAN THOMAS: You must endeavour to feel and weigh the shape, sound, content of each word in relation to the shape, sound, content etcetera of the words surrounding [before] it. It isn't only the meaning of the words that must develop harmonically...but the noise [sounds]...they make in the air and the ear, the contours in which they lie on the page and the mind, their colours and density.

In one of her poems, Emily Dickinson writes: "'Shall I take thee?' the poet said [to] / the propounded word / A. 'Be stationed with the candidates / Till I have further tried.'"

> JOHN CIARDI, *the poet*: The good poet is defined by the choices he makes... by the exactness of his demands, by the rigidity of his refusal to make cheap choices.

Emphasis should be placed on the fact that the poet chooses his or her new words more as sensory language than as semantic language—the poet pays more attention to the physical and sonal aspects of language, to the sensory qualities of words than to their content, although he or she also must pay attention to that content. The poet mentally tests words to see if they will fit the abstract rhythm, at the same time making sure that the language does not contradict the sense that has already been laid down.

The word in poetry has three functions: 1) to fill in and carry out the rhythm of the first line—this is a purely musical function; 2) to be a presence in itself—for its textural and sensory reality; and 3) (only third) to possess verbal reality—to further whatever meaning has been achieved thus far.

Theodore de Banville, a French poet: "Poetry...[is] that sorcery by which ideas are necessarily communicated to us, in a definite way, by words which nevertheless do not express them."

The language of poetry is experimental because it gives the reader a direct experience of language by providing sensations from language.

Although a word that comes to the poet's mind may have a sensory beauty by itself, it still may not be a fit word for three reasons: 1) it may not tally with the rhythm (e.g., it may be longer or shorter than the rhythm demands); or 2) it may not tally in sense with the previous sense of the poem; or 3) it may not tally in sense with the verbal consistency of the previous words. For these reasons, the verbal technique of poetry—the choice and selection of words—has to be done piecemeal—call by call, letter by letter, and syllable by syllable—and these words are needle-and-threaded harmonistically yet liquidly.

The importance of the verbal situation arises from:

1. With this summoning of language in accordance with the abstract rhythm—you are creating the physical musculature—the muscular system, the physical flesh and body of the poem.

2. With this same language, you are creating the innervation and interior nervous system for the poem—you are putting in a

network of tensions—you are endowing the poem with line nerves.

3. You are also creating a circulatory system of sounds, images and semantic meanings, weaving back and forth through metaphors and sensory values.

4. Through this same language, you are erecting an intellectual backbone, the intellectual reason of the poem.

The new words springing from the sensory consistency of the first line must have a sensory affinity with those first words. In the first line, there is already a particular alphabetic configuration of consonants and vowels. This particular alphabetic configuration produces two distinct but blended consistencies: *first*, a consistency or pattern of the same letters, consonants or vowels; and *second*, a sonal or auditory pattern—a phonology of similar sounds. This consistency of the same letters, consonants or vowels and this auditory pattern form the harmonics, the verbal reality of poetic language. This is what may be called the "hereness" of poetry—its very presence and reality—based on the physical earthiness of language.

The rhythms of the first line provide the melody; the correlations of letters and sounds provide the harmonics of poetry. Every consonant, every vowel and every letter in the first line has the potential and energy to generate further words. That is why William Blake said: "Poetry admits not a letter that is insignificant." The right words are there but you must woo them or tease them out.

In your first line, the words you already have are pregnant with potential words, with new formulations of the same letters and sounds. The further lines you need are there in the first line in a game of hide and seek.

From the first line, there is a sensory, organic sequence foreseeable not only by the eye but also by the ear, from the letters and sounds already present. The letters may change places and the sounds may change places; the letters or sounds may be shuffled, or there may be crossings and variations and new tunes with the same letter or letters, and combinations and repetitions—all of this to create correspondence with language that came before. And there may be displacement by some new letter or sound—the introduction of a new letter or sound—but there can still be a basic internal homogeneity despite the displacements.

New formations and new tunes evolve—but they will evolve from the same initial sensory and organic qualities—so that the organic nature of the growth of the poem is not destroyed, so that words are confederated, and the new formations are, therefore, simply refractions and reflections, permutations and re-combinations of the original words in the first line.

Although the poet works seriously, it is again the spirit of play.

The corresponding and responding elements give rise to resemblances. The words of the first line are like cells—which divide and reproduce new cells—and the new cells have a similar organic consistency, the same primary conformation as the parent words. They have a collective consistency, a harmonic confederacy in sound and texture—a homogenous order, a verbal and musical movement which is synchronous.[31]

The poet does not deploy the letters or sounds of the first line—but he or she sticks to them—in order to build up a language that is in correlation and in synchrony, to give the poetic line its organic rightness and keep it in character—so that there is a homogenous and confederated consistency.

By making words sound-related and letter-related, you create this correspondence—you create a choreographed language—a truly imaginative projection of language.

This is why prose is heterogeneous, a hodge-podge of verbal quality because there is no somatic relation between words, only semantic relations.

The poet cannot contravene the direction of the verbal line of force. He or she follows its genetic information to trigger new language, and this achieves a filiation of language consisting of letters, sounds and words, what Auden called the sense of "words talking among themselves."

> ROLAND BARTHES, *literary critic and philosopher*: Language is a skin: I rub my language against the other. It is as if I had words instead of fingers, or fingers at the tip of my words. My language trembles with desire.

The material teaches the artist.

Coordination of both letters and of sounds is important—but sonal correlation is more important as an excess in correlation of letters can result in just cleverness. In serious writing, you have no wish to be clever. It will result in obtrusive playfulness, which is good only for light verse. Excessive inbreeding can result in hemophilia, as in the royal families of Europe.

---

31 You should refer back to the R.P. Blackmur poem "MISSA VOCIS" on page 111 for an example of new words evolving from previous letters and sounds, and for Villa's marginal notations to that effect.

In George Wagner's pure poem in footnote 19, page 52; the playfulness was correlation of letters and sounds that was just right, and does not downgrade the lyricism of the poem.

Alliteration—which is an aspect of correlation of letters at the beginning of words—is a very obvious use and therefore not advisable. Algernon Charles Swinburne, who has poems in *A Pocket Book of Modern Verse* starting at 98, was a poet who alliterated overly, so that is why he is unread today.

Assonance—or sonal correlation within the words—is what produces the best result. See D. Thomas' "Fern Hill" (Ibid., 569).

Language, music and craft are the high tests for poetry. If the verbal situation is absent, the flesh of the poetry is absent; if the music is absent, the blood of poetry is absent. If craft is absent, the art of poetry is absent.

Texture—is the result of the poet's careful attention to verbal consistency—there is now not only a language that communicates and makes sense, but there is also an aesthetic surface, a surface that detains and arrests us. A surface is aesthetic when we are held by it and can linger over it with pleasure because it is exciting and interesting—it grabs our minds. As Robert Graves said: "Prose engages a small part of the reader's attention; poetry *all of it*."

Poetry uses verbal helicopter technique—unlike the airplane of prose, which wants to get somewhere, poetry wants to linger. Poetry also has depth power—poetry is examinable in small units—we can examine and obtain excitement letter by letter, syllable by syllable, phrase by phrase, line by line. We can go extremely local in poetry instead of by express, so there is enjoyment in every minute part of the ride. There is a weave and feel to the fabric of language—a traction that holds us down.

## CHAPTER TWENTY-TWO

# The Semantic Situation

All of the chromosomes needed to grow the poem are in the first line. Robert Frost: "Like a piece of ice on a hot stove, the poem must ride *on its own melting.*" The ride consists of the musical, verbal and semantic lines of force, musical and verbal lines of force being the major game of poetry. And yet they are not the whole game—unless you are writing pure poetry.

Every word carries inside it a meaning—sometimes clandestine. A line of verse is always to a certain extent a cage for thought. There's a sense behind the sound. Meaning is there, inside the word—standing by and ready for the poet's call. The poet will call on his or her words to release certain meanings. Until then, the words are tight-lipped. Gertrude Stein's language was very tight-lipped because she suppressed its meanings.

Poetry = language-thinking (the hyphenated word being a noun), meaning poetry produces language (in order to conjure up language for the body of the poem). If you omit the hyphen, and say: Poetry = language thinking (where language is the noun and thinking is the verb) you have the second step in the process of writing a poem, which is that in poetry language produces meaning, or language in the process of thinking out meaning. It is the language thinking, not the mind as in prose.

This is why *meaning* in poetry arrives *subconsciously*—because it is the language that is thinking and not your mind. That is what Wallace Stevens called the "special thinking of poetry."

In step one, your eyes and ears, your sensory senses, summon up and propose new words for use in the poem.

In step two, your mind—your sense of logical thinking—will decide and reject, or decide and accept—words brought forth in step one. The words you will reject—although they satisfy the correlations of letters and sounds necessary—are those words that do not promote or satisfy the logical sense of the previous words. You cannot allow the *non-sequiturs* of thought.

The verbal situation (about correlations of letters and sounds) discussed in Chapter 21 was about step one (language-thinking—with a hyphen)—which taught us how to produce more language. We will now turn to step two, which will teach us how to produce meaning.

The poetic process is not only the art of discovery of language and form (craft), but also the art of discovering meaning through language and form: it is also idea searching.

The poet uses language as a probe—as an instrument to ferret out not only form but meaning as well. The physical and sensuous poem goes in search of insight. The external poem (the poiema) goes in search of the internal poem (the logos).

The logos of the poem is its depth grammar, as the poiema is its surface grammar.

> GEORGE BARKER: I don't think the meaning is all that important, but it's one of the difficulties that make the writing of poetry as fascinating as it is.

Within the extrinsic glove of language throbs the hand called meaning.

A poem picks up thought as it goes along but it is still exploratory of meaning until the final line occurs. In poetry, you do not get a semantic answer until the poem is finished. All of its elements are in flux and merely tentative—they do not crystallize until the end of the poem.

When meaning comes, it is truly involuntary on the poet's part—whatever meaning arrives was just flushed into being by the activity of the language. The meaning was an achievement of language and the poetic art.

A poem can lead anywhere and you cannot predict where and how it will end. Poetry is not only a tightrope walk—but a blindfolded one.

> ROBERT FROST: There was that thing about every poem, I didn't see until I got to it.... I go in to see if I can get out.

Although, as mentioned before, the semantic line of force is the weakest of the three lines of force, paradoxically it is this line of force that will give depth and power to the poem. Whatever depth or insight the poem will have will spring from the semantic force.

Great poetry can arise only from the value of the semantic impact. The weight of the poet's greatness can be found in the semantic lines.

From musical and verbal felicity can spring only minor poems, although they may be of very great beauty, such as poems of Cummings, D. Thomas, John Crowe Ransom, Robert Herrick, Thomas Campion. We can call their works "high art" but not "great art," and we have the great major poets such as Hopkins, Donne, Wilfred Owen, George Herbert and Richard Eberhart.

When we emphasize the great major poets (for their great semantic force), that does not mean that they are weak in musical and verbal felicity. Above their musical and verbal felicity and beyond looms their spiritual and intellectual power, which can only be exhibited semantically.

In Chapter 14, we discussed poiema and logos. The former is the measure of the poet as artist; the latter the measure of the poet as man.

As the poet adds further words to his or her poem, the meaning is moved along, so that as the poem grows, it attains a deepening intelligence and acquires an intellectual tug. As you proceed with the poem, you will see some things falling together and you will push some more forward—until all things in the poem pull together. Fortunately, the good poet is blessed with a radar system for making sense.

The poet must keep track of what he or she has said before and every new word added must have a possible tie-in, some semantic correspondence with the previous logic—or the poem will derail.

The words of poetry cross breed not only texturally and sonally, but give you a wide choice semantically.

In writing poems, you consider words for their semantic value to the poem but those words may not fit with, and conflict with, the rhythm of the poem. This conflict is called *resistance in art*, discussed at pages 86–88 above. Every true artist welcomes this resistance because where there is no resistance there is no art. It is by overcoming this resistance of the medium that one proves oneself as an artist. The poet is he or she who can balance and reconcile these opposing forces. The poet must achieve a conciliation between the forces of music, language and meaning until there is a balancing between all three energies.

And so careful adjustments and settlements, reciprocal concessions between word and rhythm, have to be made.

Meaning moves by full words; rhythm moves by syllables. The poet is dealing more with syllables than with words because rhythm entails dealing with syllables. To affect their conciliation into a perfect event is the task of the poet.

> JOHN CROWE RANSOM: The meaning employs the words, but the meter employs not the words but the syllables. There is no point-to-point coordination between the development of the semantic structure and that of the phonetic structure. The relation between the two in a poetic phrase seems something like the relation between two melodies in counterpoint, except that our two structures uniformly look more heterogeneous than the melodies.... It seems a tighter job, stronger, and more wonderful, than the

counterpoint can be, for the melodies are two, though they are simultaneous, while the poetic phrase is a single event.

T.S. Eliot, on right language: "It is the complete consort dancing together." Poetry is not dancing to music; it is dancing the music. Meaning is only important as it becomes music.

**Figure 13.** In the diagram below, the concrete musical force is concrete because there are already words actually sounding. There is also an abstract verbal force, abstract because it does not consist of words yet, but the poet is still testing for words. The abstract musical force is without words, but is waiting for words. At the point (indicated by the arrow), where the abstract verbal force and the abstract semantic force intersect at the line of the abstract musical force, all of them become concrete. This is the way the poem develops.

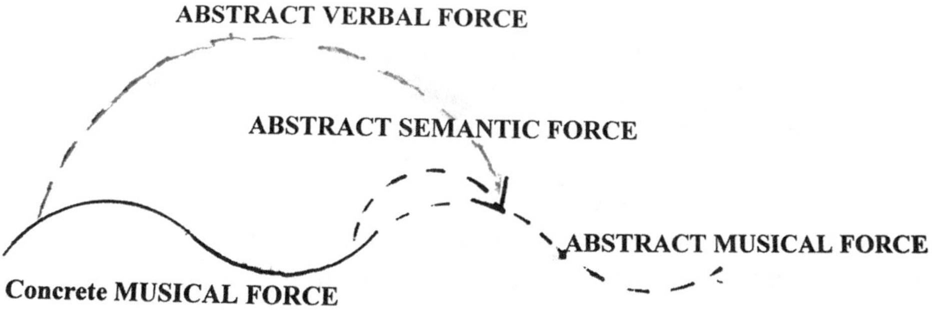


The poem discovers from inside itself what it wants to be and what it wants to mean. The poem will lead you to where it wants to go—to its inner truth. Jacques Maritain: This is what is called "organic decorum"—"the complete loyalty of a work of art to a shaping principle within itself." Paul Valéry: "A true poet will nearly always sacrifice [thought] to form (which is, after all, the end and the act [of poetry] itself)."

## CHAPTER TWENTY-THREE

# The Craft of Versification

### VERSIFICATION GENERALLY

In order to cope with the versic necessities of the poem, there must be a versic force within the poet. For, although the poem grows itself musically, verbally and semantically from the first line, as discussed above, it cannot grow itself in terms of craft. The poet must supply the craft. And without that proper execution, you have no art.

In this book, we will be teaching high technique or virtuoso technique.

If we were to paraphrase Dylan Thomas—the force (lyric poetry) that through the green fuse (technical crafting of poetic language) drives the flower (the poem)—he is asserting that technique is an essential part of the process of writing a good poem.

Versification is the way your lines are laid out and spaced out on the page. It is the challenge of form. It makes the pattern on the page. Urgency is at the core of creative movement.

Versic technique creates a serialized line—a line that ends at a suspension point—to be continued on the next line.

Movement is the adroit fingering of the lines by the poetic ear, in order not to break them but to turn them. The ear, the musical sense, chooses the line break so that, in a sense, the lines are self-regulated.

After the first line is set down on paper, whatever follows must proceed as versification.

Versification is the performance act of making verse: It is a method of construction so that the result is technically right at each and every moment, as it grows into final form.

Technique is a "performative act" as well as a performing act. The latter denotes the performance of an act already previously created. A performative act not only performs but as it acts its way along in the very moments its performance is formative, i.e., is creating the work. It creates form as it performs, so that the work consists of two elements: the working out that organically grows the work and the work itself. Thus the arts of theatre and dance are performing acts. In dance, the work of the choreographer is performative. The poetic process is performative, while the prose process is simply performing.

The poet as he writes has his or her eye out for every chance to exploit the possibilities of construction—for the act of writing is the very occasion and discovery of form.

Every true poet realizes that the perfection of poetry resides in the versification, for versification is the very art of poetry.

To write in verse means to manipulate the verse-line, to be concerned with its movements and tensions, to be concerned with the effects of craft. Versification is the motor of form. Therefore, versification should be the first and most active principle in poetry writing. Every poet should know how to moderate his or her line—because versification is the art of lineation, the art of line structure, the art of hewing and carving of verse lines. It is the art of knowing how and when to begin and end or continue a line. Every good poet runs a risk—to enable a line to go so far but only that far and no farther.

Because he or she is line-toeing each line so that every line is in place and no line is out of joint, the poet must construct the verse-line, with its tension and movement, as a unit of structure.

Versification is the finger work of poetry—Robert Frost: "The way you lay your sentences in your stanzas."

Poetry is the art of the broken line—if the lines were not broken in poetry, you would not have verse. Apart from the breaking of lines, the line has a lot of "local" interference—it cannot move a step ahead, or even a letter ahead, without the musical, verbal, semantic and tensional elements demanding their due.

Versification is the instrument of poetry as language is its material. The true poet plays his or her craft more than anything else: energetic engagement with the medium, moment-to-moment-to-moment in virile thrusts on the page.

When you are "technicalizing" your poem with correct versification, you are energizing it, winding energy up into the poem, so that it becomes a highly-charged object. With each line that is well-tooled and carved out, the poem coils up more upsurge, more current, by which to turn the poem into a miracle.

The poet deals with resistances by language, by rhythm, by meaning, and these resistances you must correlate. Versification always means creating resistances. The excellence of a poem lies in its resistances. Things must resist us when we want to do them, so that they can resist time when it wants to undo them.

Although language brings in sounds, the music is only potential until the right versification comes. This is because sounds are different from music. And different versifications will produce different kinds of music. For it is versification that controls the movement of the sounds—it does not alter the sounds of the syllables but it can alter the movement, the rhythm of the syllables by the length of the technical line. Different versifications carry different movements—but there is a right movement for any particular set of language.

Versification is, then, the "conducting" by the poet of his or her language and music. In poetry, you are both the composer and the conductor of the music of your language—you conduct by your adeptness in versification.

Versification also gives the writing a hard edge. It gives the poem a bounding line—it shapes the figure of the poem—it puts a skin tight over your language so that the poem's flesh is shaped up. It gives the poem a profile, a figure, a silhouette—making the figure of the poem stand out in clear definition.

The subtleties of craft provide the poem with facets, as in a diamond, so that the poem has refractions and brilliances. The poem has been brought out in high relief—it has been chiseled line by line into contour and shapeliness.

Poetic excitement is: first, linguistic and sensory excitement and then it becomes and is always, second, versic excitement.

Versification accomplishes form in poetry—it lights up the form of the poem and shows us the beauty of limits and discipline. It is this radiant actuality of form that constitutes art.

C.S. Lewis said: "[A]n appreciation of sculpture which ignored the statue's shape in favor of the sculptor's 'view of eye' would be self-deceptive. It is by the shape that it is a statue. Only because it is a statue do we come to be mentioning the sculptor's view of eye at all."

In poetry, although versification's main function is to create the proper movement of tension and music, versification also serves to keep the medium in motion and, at the same time, cool and poised under control.

## LINE MOVEMENT

Versification sets the speed of the line—by regulating the length of the line. This creates the lineal movement. The length of the line will govern the undulations of movement from line to line. The movement of lines can be made either more active or less active according to the line length: short lines have more activity than longer lines, but require more dexterity in craft. Longer lines have less activity because the activity of movement usually occurs at the end of the line.

The proper versification gives the poem energy and bounce quite apart from the energy of the subject or meaning. It gives the poem a technical focus. Robert Frost: "Our technique becomes as much material as material itself."

A good example is Marianne Moore's poem "The Fish" with its dazzling footwork, full of verbal plies and pirouettes, a series of technical knockouts, a spritely and adroit balletic movement (where Cummings is merely gymnastic).[32]

D. THOMAS: The form springs up urgently as the temper of making needs it.

---

32 Villa stated to the Editor that he learned his technique of versification from reading and studying the poems of Hopkins, Cummings, and Marianne Moore. From the poems of these three, he said, he learned handling of language, handling of the poetic line, and the tensions involved. As each poem will demand its individual technique and growth, in accordance with its needs, the poems of these three poets should be carefully studied *technically* by anyone who is serious about poetry and wishes to understand and develop the craft that is the subject of this Chapter. As reported at the end of Chapter 18, footnote 27, the complete poems of two of these poets, Hopkins and Cummings, were read by Villa in each of the years in which he was writing his poetry.

Another way of self-teaching the methods of versification advocated in this book is to obtain the Penguin Classics Centennial Edition of Villa's collected poems published in celebration of Villa's August 5, 1908 birth: John Edwin Cowen, ed., *José Garcia Villa—Doveglion* (pseud.)*: Collected Poems* (New York: Penguin Group, 2008). Commencing at 147 is a discussion by Villa of the concept of "Adaptations"—poems that he constructed in verse from prose materials (and sometimes bad verse)—together with adaptations he so constructed. Villa utilized adaptation assignments as homework in his Poetry Workshop III as a means of teaching versification through practice. In the Appendix on Adaptations below, I have set forth the assignment sheet Villa distributed to workshop members, specifying the guidelines governing students' responses to these assignments.

When one fully understands the adaptation process, he or she can scout out additional material with which to practice versification.

You can change the movement of a line by breaking it at a different word than where it presently ends. Hypothetically, you can break the line at any word of the sentence, and turn the line there—and it will cause a change in movement. I say "hypothetically," because there is however only one true point where it can turn best, to serve the necessities of the poem.

Versification also locks up the line at the line break; it immobilizes the line at that particular point. This is necessary not only to create tension, but for the form and pattern of the poem to emerge—to etch out the poem's contours and figure.

Thus, we see that versification involves not only a musical but an athletic skill craft. Naturally it is full of dangers—but the good poet manages beautiful escapes.

> MARIANNE MOORE: Ecstasy affords the occasion and *expediency* determines the form.

Expediency means doing what is advantageous at that particular moment, under the circumstances.

Technique is not just one move but a constant series of moves that build up, add up, and finally consolidate. You make a venture at every chance that presents itself. In this way the poet makes technical discoveries as he proceeds. As he searches out the musical framework for the poem, he discovers new erogenous zones for the poem.

In order to be able to do this, we must acquire technical mastery—because that is what versification is. Paul Valéry defined "mastery" thus:

> ... to have command over the technical resources of an art...The acquisition of mastery...presupposes the acquired habit of always thinking... with the technical means as point of departure, and of never thinking of a work except in terms of its [technical] means.

## INTERLINEAL AND INTERSTANZAIC MOVEMENT

**Figure 14.** Villa utilized the following diagram to demonstrate how the poem moves from line to line and from stanza to stanza:

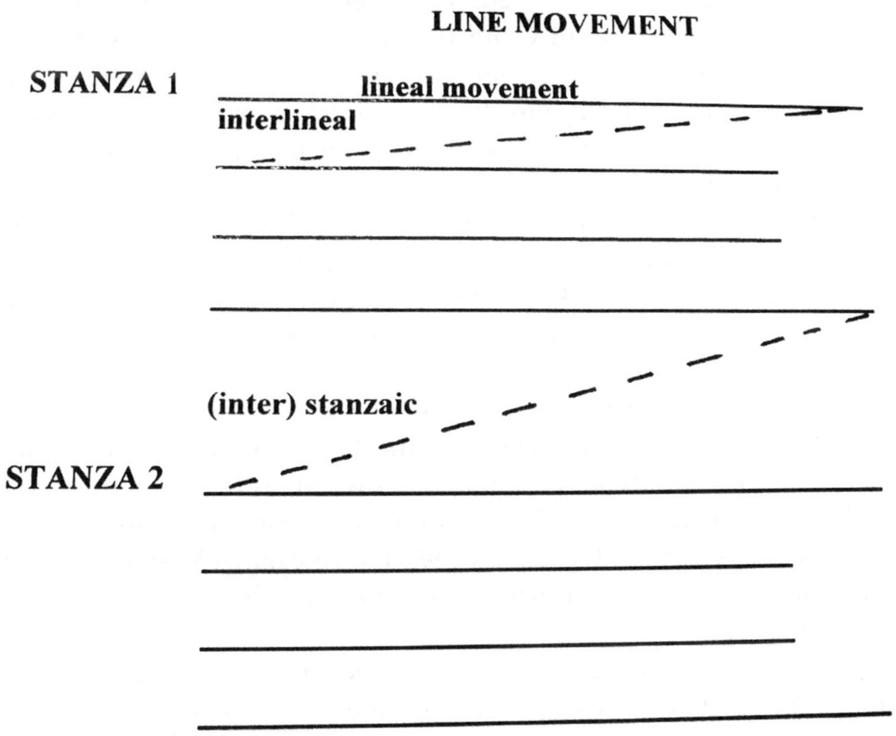


The setting of the speed of the line, by regulating the length of the line, creates its lineal movement. Versification is the art of locking up this lineal movement by creating the right line break (necessary for the form and pattern) and at the same time releasing the movement toward the next line. At the same time that versification locks up the line—locks up the lineal movement—immobilizes it to create tension—it also releases the temporary lock and springs the line forward to the next line, so that the movement is unbroken. The locking up and concurrent release of the lock through the line break constitutes the interlineal movement of the verse. It enables the verse-line to "turn round the corner" to the next line—to turn with dexterity as well as music. In Marianne Moore's "The Fish," this interlineal movement is achieved with split-second tactics.

You shape the line musically and tensionally before you shape it visually. The musical-tensional determination is what determines the line's visual shape.

The poet turns the corner with the right word—sometimes the right part of the word—as if there were no corner there. As a result, instead of angularity we get a limpidity and plasticity of movement, a soft round edge. In this movement of turning the corner, the poet is—in one simultaneous act—dancer (for it must be done gracefully), sculptor (the poet is etching the shape of the poem), and athlete (he or she is moving ably and at the nick of time).

Turning the corner means dovetailing the individual verse lines—providing the gap between any two lines with a connective tension—so that there is a wholeness to the language and an undisturbed continuity to the movement. It means avoiding fractures or cracks in the fabric of poetry, i.e., damage to the medium.

"Verse" derives from the Latin word *versus*—to turn around. The purpose of versification is to achieve linkage, a cohesion, so that there is a continuous surface and a supple life running through the lines. The result of such management is a flexibility and resilience, a line sinuous and lithe and viable and also bends without breaking. With this quality of tensile strength, there is then a live connection between lines instead of a dormant gap.

This brings us to the *pivot word*, the end-word of the line. The location of the pivot word is a very strategic and pivotal point in the writing of verse. It is this pivot word that end-locks the line (for the form's sake) but only temporarily for, at the same time, it releases the rhythm for the movement's sake that it may go on to the next line. The pivot word has the positional control and responsibility for movement and tension—and so acts also as a cohesive factor keeping the medium intact, whole and unfractured.

The line stops only visually—it doesn't stop time. The end-word of a free verse line is a stop-time word: the line snaps off because the word is non-pivoting.

The pivot word enables the line to move with hairline precision—gives the line the quality of jeweled performance. Now the lines read not only from left to right but also from right to left because of the swivel effect. Therefore, it is by the rightness and quality of his or her pivot words (line ends) that you can judge the quality of the poet. What the poet is seeking is a series of right entrances and exits through pivotal words, which is particularly present in the works of Marianne Moore.

The pivot word enables the new line to slip easily in and the old line to slip gracefully out. There is a cushioned break of the line, and there is a cushioned movement. The poet makes a snake of language, its body supple. Without the pivot word, the lines would be like still photographs, like a slide show. With the pivot word, the lines flow together like motion pictures because they are in flux and motion.

Pivot words form a buffer zone that ultimately decides pattern and shape of the stanza, as well as the movement of the stanza.

Poems fail, at a low level, because the writer was not aware of the poetic necessities, or at a high level, because the writer was aware of the poetic necessities and was unable to satisfy them.

## STANZATION

Versification concerns not only the pivot word, the proper turning of the line, but also the building of the stanza, or stanzation.

The line is the technical unit for the movement of the poem. The stanza is the technical unit for the structure of the poem, the building block of which the verse line is only a sub-unit.

When the first stanza is completed, poetry suddenly becomes not only audio-verbal but also audio-visual. You have now given the sounds of poetry a graphic visage, a face, a visual countenance. The creation of the stanza has created a special physiognomy for the poem—a particular choreographic formation of the lines.

When you had only lines that were incomplete as stanza, the poem had no face yet, no visual character. Only at the completion of the first stanza did the poem begin to have a specific shape and look. The poem now has not only completed but discovered its basic structural unit—and this stanza has an individual visage and shape. You have now created a pattern—the visual arrangement and pictorial order—that gives the poem a tidy order, a satisfying neatness of form—a sense of governed order and balance of neat design. Technical order and tensional order have now been gathered into one visual and structural order.

It is the pattern that creates the lyric form, absent in blank verse and in free verse. Poetry is the design and balance of verbal language. The poem as it proceeds is discovering not only its meaning but also its form—and the form is the form that the poem itself wants to take—by demand of its internal necessities. The stanza is not imposed from without but organically grows and designs itself, with the aid of the pivot words.

Now the poem, by its employment of the stanza, achieves and attains elements of performance and fixity because that is what the pattern does:

it fixes permanently the shape of the poem. And the stanza has elements of energy, tension, motion and direction—because that is what the verse-corners (the pivot words) do—they make lines culminate at strategic points.

The first stanza is complete as soon as the technical, musical and tensional necessities of that part of the poem are fulfilled. It does not require semantic or syntactic fulfillment—that is, completion of the thought or sentence. The technical form and pattern of the stanza is completed when the poet cannot add another word or syllable to the pattern without damaging and infringing upon the movement.

Because the thought of the poem is still incipient, the poet has no intent to work to complete a thought. The poem, worked out by the poetic process, is being formed by the language and the technical demands of versification.

The stanza does not break movement but strengthens and vitalizes it. Although each stanza is visually isolated, its very isolation dramatically and technically intensifies interconnections.

The poet usually repeats the same (stanza) pattern until the poem is complete. The first stanza becomes the model stanza—and its line lengths should be matched in the corresponding lines of the following stanza. That is, unless the poem chooses to have a compound pattern for the sake of movement and tension.

You can balance the pattern in any of three ways or their combinations: 1) by having an even visual equivalence length of the corresponding lines, 2) by having the same number of words in each line; and/or 3) by having the same number of syllables in each line. You should choose the alternative(s) that gives the best movement to the line, in consonance with the previous movement.

Here you see that the stanza is not only a formal pattern for aesthetic form, but also somewhat of a mathematical pattern to give precision to that aesthetic form.

The second stanza is more difficult to write than the first stanza. You will find greater resistance by language in stanza 2 (as in all subsequent stanzas). The pattern of the first stanza grows organically from the demands of tension, rhythm and language, but now the new language you have must fit into a pattern not of its own making. For the ensuing stanzas, the poet needs control and adjustments.

A stanza may be composed of any number of lines—the number being dictated by the structural and dramatic tension evolving. You may even have a one-word stanza, as the following poem of Gloria Guy, one of my students, illustrates:

**Figure 15.**

only mention

this

'cause I have to

watch

you make your

own

cocoon and

hatch

— Gloria Guy

## SUSPENSION

In multi-stanza poems, stanzation serves three functions:

1. Creation of the proper poetic tension and movement through the principle of suspension, suspension of language and suspension of the meaning. Stanzation creates pauses in space for the eye as well as pauses in time for tension—it creates a dialogue between occupied space and vacant space in dynamic inaction so that there is a leavening as in cakes or bread. Instead of a messy dough, you obtain a lightness that adds value.

2. Serves to aerate, to oxygenate the poem—the poem is allowed to come up for light and air but also poetical respiration, instead of congestion and suffocation.

3. Sets the principle of visual design, of visual lyric form—is good to look at.

Suspension is the technique of withholding the content through the structure, and vice versa—of unfolding content slowly, by means of delays and complications, by providing hold-backs. One element pushes the poem forward while another holds it back so that each line is at razor's edge, so that a sense of imminence grows—and the mind is waiting for something.

The purpose, therefore, is to raise anticipation and expectancy in the reader, so that the poem will have greater tension and ultimately a greater final impact. It is the brinkmanship of literary cliffhanging—of keeping things teetering on the verge as on the edge of a cliff—so that when the pressure of suspension is released, there is a sudden change of meaning.

The three elements of suspension are: 1) achieving the high note, 2) delay, and 3) disclosure.

On the principle of delaying for a purpose, for the purpose of disclosure, suspension is built. It is basically the art of drama—which always moves on the delayed action process. It is a technical device to heighten up the drama of the poem. It's really the same principle as that of striptease.

Suspension is the way you build up suspense before you make your disclosure. Example: "The hardest bed in the world... / to get out of."

A poem is not only a collection of phrases but must show a dramatic, structural energy—there must be a heightening of pressures; otherwise, there is flatness.

Versification, through the pivot word, creates boundaries of tension as well as boundaries of shape—so that the verse lines are in a state of flexion and tension—so that every line is a clenched fist, with a thrust and parry. When this tension is present, you have the poetic pitch of poetry. Without this tension, you have only a watery lingual soup, as in free verse discussed in Chapter 11.

Primarily, suspension means dramatizing the technique—tightening the technical vise of the verse, so that there is the pull of the line against the pull of the sense, a tug-of-war between these forces. The pull against each other creates aesthetic steam because at the same time there is a continuity and opposition, flexion and tension, creating an undertow of drama. You could say the art of poetry lives close to the nerve.

The kinds of structural suspension available to the poet are:

1. *Linear suspension* – suspension within a line and achieved by means of the right punctuation, e.g., the comma, the dash, the colon, the semi-colon, or simply a wider space. (A hyphen is very bad for poetry.) You must hear punctuation in poetry; you can hear everything—words, pauses, blank spaces, as well as punctuation. Thus, in poetry, punctuation is not primarily used as in prose for clarity, as clarity is of secondary importance in poetry, but is used to regulate the movement of the poem.

2. *Inter-linear suspension* – where the line itself terminates at a strategic point and you can think of a pivot word as nerve-stretching. You endow the lines with a *perils-of-Pauline*, nick-of-time, element so that your language is writhing tissue, seething with drive. What is suspended is the important or the impacted word or phrase, which is delayed to the next line.

3. *Indentional suspension* – also an interlinear (between lines) suspension, i.e., it is from one line to the next but it effects more modulations than are possible with the simple interlinear suspension. By indenting the line to the right or projecting it out to the left,[33] the speed of movement is altered, as well as by the distance of the indentation or projection. You should realize that the moment you indent, you're making your pattern sharper. Indentations give the poem an East-West axis—just as stanza patterns give the poem a North-South axis. Modulation

33 The latter, Villa referred to as "outventing."

of tone can also be effected by the use of either capital or lower-case letters.

4. *Stanzaic suspension* – where the suspension is from one stanza to the next. What is suspended again is the important or impacted word or phrase.

**Figure 16.** As illustrated by the following diagram, indentional suspensions and outventings of lines effect more modulation of tone than is possible with just straight margins, through altering the speed of the motion from line to line. The greater the distance the eye travels from one line to the next, the slower the motion, whereas the shorter the distance, the faster the motion. This is subject to the *caveat* that the indentation or outventing must visually look all right as well.

**STRAIGHT MARGIN**

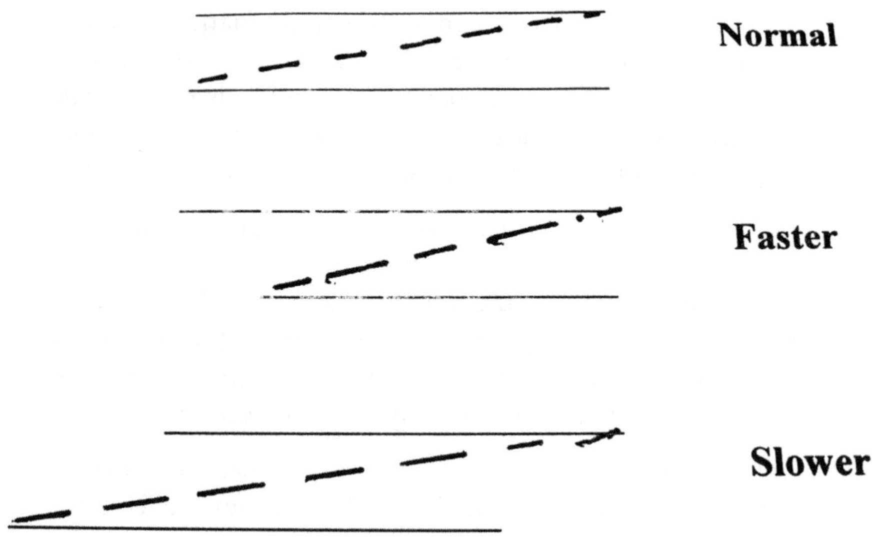


Indention differs from indentation in prose and poetry. In prose, we indent to form a new paragraph but we do not accomplish a suspension of movement. In versification, the indention and outvention suspend the movement of the verse—hence the indention results in indentation. Outvention differs from indentation in that the further you extend the line to the left, the longer the pause. Thus, in poems, indention and outvention have opposite effects.

How does the poet decide whether to use stanzaic suspension instead of interlinear suspension? In general, the poet first uses interlinear suspensions. When the poet needs a longer (in point of time) move, a more dramatic suspension, when it's time for a major move, then it is time for a stanzaic suspension. This major suspension decides when the stanza is over. Suspension may sequester a whole line by itself—for the best dramatic impact and this organically creates for the poem a second or compound pattern.

A good poem not only has an organized pattern of sound and language, but also an organized pattern of silence.

A compound pattern may be resolved in three ways: 1)following the same order of structure—see, e.g., the Gloria Guy poem on page 133 and see her poem *slowly, like a shade* below; 2) following the reverse order of structure—e.g., a five-line stanza followed by a 1-line stanza, where another 1-line stanza follows and the poem is closed with another five-line stanza; or 3) adding another stanza of identical pattern as the first stanza after a second stanza with a different pattern.

Thus, if you have four lines in your first stanza and two lines in the second (for the sake of movement), you have a pattern 1) if your third stanza has four lines and your fourth has two lines, or 2) if your third stanza has two lines and your fourth has four lines, or 3) if your third stanza has four lines, your fourth stanza has two lines and the fifth stanza has four lines. However, 4) if your third stanza has four lines and you have no fourth stanza, that is not an acceptable pattern.

A *non*-pattern is unacceptable, such as where you follow a five-line first stanza only with two 1-line stanzas, or you follow two five-line stanzas with a one 1-line stanza.

What is important, in addition to movement, is a sense of design and balance.

**Figure 17.** The following poem, "slowly like a shade," written by my student Gloria Guy, has a progressive pattern, which is an acceptable pattern.[34]

**slowly, like a shade**

understand why-so, so
slowly, like a shade

the son, the daughter
understand why-so, so
slowly, like a shade

winding now it seems
the son, the daughter
understand why-so, so
slowly, like a shade

nor shameful is that
winding now it seems
the son, the daughter
understand why-so, so
slowly, like a shade

long, white in waves
nor shameful is that
winding now it seems
the son, the daughter
understand why-so, so
slowly, like a shade

allow a letting down
long, white in waves
nor shameful is that
winding now it seems
the son, the daughter
understand why-so, so
slowly, like a shade

---

34 The first stanza is one line, the second is two lines, etc. It follows the same order of structure from top to bottom, and there is a repetition of the same lines adding a new one to each stanza. The structure has the additional virtue of being a visual representation of a shade being slowly lowered.

Such a poem could be started with a number of lines and end with one line, so long as the pattern is progressive. The repetition of the same lines is not necessary, as in the Guy poem. Also, you could start with one line and progress to several lines and then progress back to one line again, so long as the lines are balanced.

## POETIC TENSION

What *suspension* achieves in poetry is *poetic tension.*

Tension is opposing forces—held in check by the form of the poem. One extra letter or syllable can crush the whole structure. In writing a poem, the language and music pull the poem outward, whereas versification pulls the poem inward.

Tension gives the lines a poetic beat. All the while the poem proceeds it is in technical and thematic fever—and gets well only at the final line. A poem is a sensuous object. Though the poem is nervous and tense while in progress, the completed poem ends a very healthy object. Without this live fever, the finished work would be a wax-word poem.

As the poem grows, there is an acceleration and escalation of tension—and poetry becomes an art of the nerves. Tension gives urgency—the quality of passionate statement.

Poetic tension refers to both the technical tension of the verse, and the tension of the feeling—the emotive tension of the sense.

Versification is a tactical method of creating not just technical tension, but rhythmic tension, semantic tension and emotional tension.

**Figure 18.** The following diagram was prepared by Villa and used by him to demonstrate the effect of tension on the language and craft of poetry:

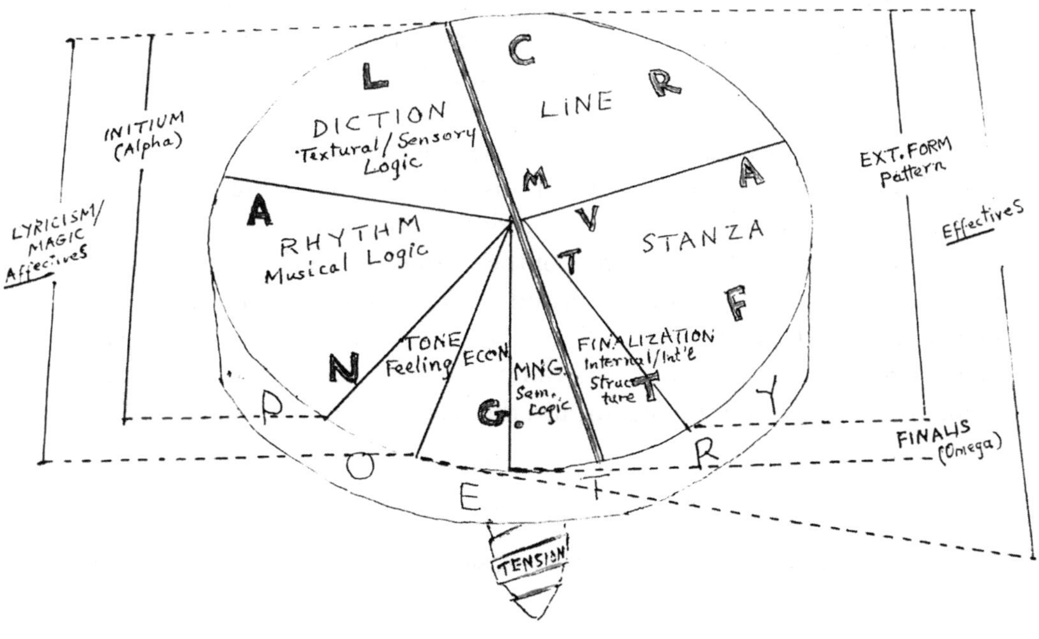

The circle of poetry is divided between poetic language and craft (technique).

The area designated as "LYRICISM/MAGIC" is characterized as "Affectives" to signify that they are the emotional, rather than intellectual, aspects of poetry. The area designated as "INITIUM (Alpha)" refers to the first line, the beginning of the poem. On the right side of the diagram, the "EFFECTIVES" is a reference to the technical intellectual effects created in the writing of the poem. Under "FINALIZATION," the "internal/int'l structure" refers to when we are moved intellectually by the poem's structure. The "FINALIS (Omega)" is a reference to the last line of the poem, its finalization where the meaning of the poem is discovered and the circuit is completed that makes the poetry a poem. See Chapter 25 below.

The "MVT" is an abbreviation of the word "movement," the tightening of tension as the poet's craft moves from line to line and from stanza to stanza, building up to finalization of the poem, which is the subject of Chapter 25. [35]

## RHYME

Pattern may also be associated with sound devices like rhyme. Rhyme is musical patterning. Where there is no repetition, there is no pattern. A poem with one stanza may be said to have no pattern.

In rhyming poems, you have rhymes at certain points and you create corresponding points in each stanza. You may complete a first stanza without a rhyme pattern as yet—and then achieve a rhyme pattern in the following stanza by rhyming the corresponding lines with those in the first stanza.

Or, you may create a mirror stanza—having the properties of a mirror, reflecting backward. Dylan Thomas, in his poem "Author's Prologue," in *A Pocketbook of Modern Verse* (553–55), composed two stanzas of 51 lines each and rhymed backward so that line 1 of the second stanza rhymed with line 51 of the first stanza, line 2 of the second stanza rhymed with line 50 of the first, and so forth all the way to line 51 of the second rhymed with line 1 of the first. The second stanza was much more difficult to write because, while the first stanza grew organically, the second stanza has to fit its language into the pattern.

---

35 This diagram, more than any other, pulls together and summarizes Villa's concept of how lyric poems are crafted.

A one stanza poem can have a pattern: a visual pattern, a rhyming pattern, or an intellectual pattern, such as a mirror poem. See, e.g., Richard Eberhart's "The Groundhog," in *Twentieth Century American Poetry* (350–51); R.P. Blackmur's "Half-Tide Ledge" (Ibid., 281); William Carlos Williams' "Portrait of a Lady" (Ibid., 133–35); in each of these dramatic poems necessity demanded tensional continuance. Or the poem may be a solid stanza with the pattern held together by a rhyme scheme, where the musical necessity demands continuance without a break. See Robert Frost's poems "Fire and Ice" and "Bereft" (Ibid., 70–72); Emily Dickinson's poems "XIV" and "A Snake" (Ibid., 11).

### IMAGINATIVE RHYME SCHEMES

Among the innovations that true poets have brought to poetry by their attention to technique and energetic engagement with the medium has been the invention of rhyme schemes other than the rhymes with which we are all familiar—e.g., "see" with "tree," "said" with "bed." Emily Dickinson used "slant rhyme" or "half rhyme"—e.g., "live" with "dive," "home" with "lime." Wilfred Owen invented consonantal rhyme, e.g., "live" with "love," "blood" with "brood," etc.[36] And Cummings, in his poem "rosetree,rosetree," invented a rhyme scheme that rhymed the last word in his first line with the second-to-last syllable of the second line, as found in E. E. Cummings, *Complete Poems 1904–1962*, George J. Firmage, ed., 763 (New York: Liveright Publishing, 1991).[37]

Richard Wilbur reflected upon the value of rhyme in the composition of a poem as follows:

> Aside from its obvious value in the finished poem as a part of poetic form and as a heightener of language, rhyme seems to me an invaluable aid in composition. It creates difficulties which the utterance must surmount

---

36 Villa invented reversed-consonance rhyme, e.g., "days" with "said," "near" with "run." José Garcia Villa, *Have Come, Am Here* (New York: Viking Press, 1942), 151–52.

37 Cummings' rhyme scheme, incidentally, went unnoticed until Villa, who always before anything else read poems technically, discovered the scheme and wrote of it to Cummings. Cummings responded with the proverb: "set a thief to catch a thief."

Many of Villa's poems utilized rhyme schemes, as did the poems of many of his contemporaries. However, Villa did not consider rhyme essential to poetic technique. The Editor cannot recall Villa ever criticizing a poem for its failure to utilize a rhyme scheme and he praised many poems that did not do so. However, Villa viewed rhyme as one of many checks and constraints or "resistances" that the poet could place in his own path so that, by overcoming them, his poems would also resist time when it wanted to undo them. See, e.g., pages 86–87 above.

by increased resourcefulness. It also helps by liberally suggesting arbitrary connections of which the mind may take advantage if it likes. For example, if one has to rhyme with tide, a great number of rhyme-words at once come to mind (ride, bide, shied, confide, etc.). Most of these, in combination with tide, will probably suggest nothing apropos, but one of them may reveal precisely what one wanted to say. If none of them does, tide must be dispensed with. Rhyme, austerely used, may be a stimulus to discovery and a stretcher of the attention.

PAUL VALÉRY: There are many more chances of a rhyme furnishing an 'idea' (literary) than of finding the rhyme from the 'idea.'[38]

38 John Felstiner, Professor Emeritus of English, Stanford University, in his book *Can Poetry Save the Earth?* (New Haven: Yale University Press, 2009), 123, tells of an occasion he attended where Robert Frost told the gathering that he received many letters from aspiring poets and that: "I open them up and if the poems haven't any rhyme I toss them right in the trash. Now, if they're rhymed, and one word belongs there for the sense while the other's dragged in to make a rhyme, I throw *them* away too. But if I can't tell which is which, if both rhyme words belong, why those are the poems I read!" The lesson is, while rhyme is far from imperative, if one chooses to rhyme one must rhyme well.

## CHAPTER TWENTY-FOUR

# Abstraction in Poetry

Poetry is essentiality and abstraction. The perceiving of the abstract belongs to the discipline of the imagination—not to the discipline of craft. A poet may have one of these disciplines without the other. For example, Marianne Moore had the discipline of craft but not the discipline of the imagination; and Richard Eberhart, on the other hand, had the discipline of the imagination but (at least in his later poems) not the discipline of craft.

To "abstractize"[39] a poem to essence is not the same thing as reducing it to "the bare bones"—because even "the bare bones" would still be too detailed. The abstract is even barer—it is the ultimate distillate of essence.

The process of abstraction is the process of simplifying from excess amplitude and disorder to unit order and essential structure. Non-essential details are honed down and eliminated for the sake of the design.

The higher the mind, the more it thinks in terms of abstraction—it weeds out all unnecessaries and inessentials—to arrive at the core structure and the core essence of things. This power comes only with the refinement of the intelligence.

In her 81st year, Marianne Moore revised her five-stanza poem "Poetry," in *Twentieth Century American Poetry* (173–74), to cut it to a one-stanza poem:

> I, too, dislike it,
> Reading it, however, with a perfect contempt for it, one dis-
> covers in
> it, after all, a place for the genuine.[40]

> WALLACE STEVENS: The momentum toward abstraction exerts a greater force on the poet than the painter. I imagine that the tendency of all thinking is toward the abstract and perhaps I am merely saying that the abstractions of the poet are abstracter than the abstractions of the painter.

39 Another Villa-coined word.

40 As published in *The Complete Poems of Marianne Moore* (New York: Viking Press, 1967), 36, with an author's note: "Omissions are not accidents. M.M."

The process of abstraction dematerializes and defactuates. The principle of abstraction is a reductive principle and simplifies things because not all details are given.

Poetry deals with essence. Therefore it must distill. Statistical elements and documentary details are distractive. Exclusions—negative space—become necessary in order to produce a distillate of positive space.

Abstraction, in effect, diagrams—it is the art of perceiving the fundamental diagram of things, of finding the essential basic structure.

But poetry is not abstraction alone. If it were, it would be like a desiccated skeleton without the breath of life. Therefore, abstraction must be blooded, must be provided with the words running blood.

> WALLACE STEVENS: Poetry is an abstraction blooded.

> LEO STEIN: It is the abstract of values expressed in the concrete of terms.

And how does the poet concretize the abstract once he has perceived it? He does it by using metaphors.

Metaphors express the abstract, the intangible—but in concrete terms. The essence of all metaphor is metaphysical, and the metaphysical is always abstract. We must realize that one element of a metaphor is always concrete. That is why Ernest Fenollosa defined metaphors as "*material* images to suggest immaterial relations...the bridge from the minor truth of *seen* to the *major* truth of the unseen."

A metaphor is footed, on one side, on a concrete fact—but its end-object is not concrete.

> LAURA RIDING: "The end of poetry is to leave everything as pure and bare as possible.... The greater the clutter attacked, and the smaller the power of the residue to which it is reduced, the better the poem.

In our study of the Spectrum of Poetry, we noted the region of pure poetry, composed of two adjacent areas: pure concrete poetry and pure abstract poetry. In pure abstract poetry—it is abstract by lack of content, as in Gertrude Stein's work. It is a true and literal abstract: a void, a vacuum, a nothingness of essence, a complete negation of meaning.

However, now, when we employ the words "abstract" and "abstraction"—there is a content involved, but this content has been reduced to its essentials, like a tree in winter.

In other words, now we are dealing with metaphysical and intellectual abstraction and this kind of abstraction is not a void or a vacuum. It is abstract only by reason that it has undergone the process of abstraction—but there *is* content.

In Gertrude Stein's work, the process of abstraction was not involved. Her work started abstract.

When the poem does not begin abstract, but starts from a mass of concreteness and then results in some abstraction, then it has been subjected to the process of abstraction.

The best poetry—or great poetry—does not start abstract, except in the sense that the good poet has nothing in his or her mind when he begins the poem. What his subconscious digs up from him (for him) is certainly not abstract, though all of this material, if he or she is a good poet, will be made abstract. It is in this process that the poem must learn sacrifice—what details to leave out for the poem's good. Every good artist has a well-functioning internal rejection mechanism.

In general, whatever does not harmonize with the sound and movement of the verse must be rejected. The lyrical musical syllables must have primacy of place at the expense of thought.

Wallace Stevens' poem: "Sea Surface Full of Clouds," in *Twentieth Century American Poetry* (111–16), begins: "In that November off Tehuantepec," He was there in October—thus the line is factually incorrect but fact was sacrificed to suit the music.

> PAUL VALÉRY: I am by no means certain that the idea which engenders the work is always the idea of the work engendered. It is perfectly possible to arrive at a different work.

> PABLO PICASSO: What a sad thing for a painter who loves blondes but denies himself the pleasure of putting them in his pictures because they don't go well with the basket of fruit. What misery for a painter who detests apples to have to use them all the time because they harmonize with the tablecloth.

However, even if things can be made to harmonize with the sound and movement of the verse, there are things that by the very nature of poetry must be excluded, which have no place at all in poetry. And, in general, these are explicit and exhaustive details—even if they are actual and true, such as the merely descriptive and enumerative details of prose, the details of external reality, of surface documentation. A factual mentality can never produce poetry.

Abstraction is factive, but not factual. Factive is of the nature of fact (which is truth).

The details of poetry are, through "abstractization," conveyed through metaphors of language, made of language and not actual details as in prose.

Metaphors are linguistic objects made of language, but which can act with great power since they act symbolically through abstraction. And this is what makes poetry a visionary labor—it dissolves the particular into the general and universal.

Abstraction removes actual representation and portrays the vital, inner structure, trimming off excesses and superficial details. Poetry is not at the information level, but at the X-ray level. Its information is inside information. Realism is for prose, reality for poetry.

> VLADIMIR NABOKOV: Life is so easy to describe, so hard to imagine.

Fortunately, for the poet, the sense of form—which makes him stick to form—helps a great deal in making eliminations of detail. Matter which does not promote the form must be discarded.

> PAUL VALÉRY: Why do I use strict form? To prevent the poem saying everything.

Where there is so much matter present, the result is usually an opacity of meaning. The work, besides being heavy and messy, becomes unclear.

Versification can aid the poet technically and to discover his or her subject. But it cannot shape up the subject in terms of logic and intellect. However, the process of "abstractization" can help the poet to structure the intellectual form of his or her poem.

By perceiving through the mass and profusion of external details, by making external reality recede, the poet arrives at only valid details that are intellectually true. This is what we call the discipline of the imagination.

Metaphors the poet inserts must rub elbows with the other metaphors inserted; they should intertwine and counterpoise; and they must complicate in one direction without branching. The poem can afford only one direction because of its intensity and economy. In the end, our intellectual structure is—and must be—also a dramatic structure, a structural unity and climax.

## ACHIEVING COMPLEXITY AND INTELLECTUAL CHALLENGE IN POETRY

The moment the poet makes his or her poem abstract, he or she is also making it more complex and intellectually challenging. One method involves the other. For the moment a thing becomes abstract, it is immaterialized—it thereby becomes more difficult to be perceived with ordinary eyes. A riddle arises and is made—and precisely because there is a riddle, the work has become more interesting and challenging. The riddle requires more intelligence to solve.

The metaphor abets this complexity by its nature of obliquity. The metaphor is a device of direction by indirection. It is Here-via-There. The "Here" element pertains to the "here" things, the concrete things, and the "There" element to the abstract relationship being pointed out obliquely by the metaphor. In the metaphor, the organic and inorganic are unified.

In summary, the metaphor enriches language, gives it more vitality, gets us to the vital essence, complexity and intellectual challenge of poetry, and concentrates and thus condenses and crystallizes the poem.

## CHAPTER TWENTY-FIVE

# Resolution and Last Line

The musical, verbal, semantic and versic forces work, not individually, but as a continuum—as a unit—as a team, for the poem's good. This produces the *archetype* or *model poem.*

A continuum is a continuity that forms a totality. It rounds itself up; it comes full circle. The continuum sets limits to the continuity so that it reaches an end and yet is not broken, because a wholeness of fabric and ambit has been organized.

A total is merely a sum—a totality is an ensemble, a unity, a resultant organized whole—a functioning closed system.

Strictly speaking, the word form should mean both external form (technique/craft) and internal form (inorganic—abstract and mental—the intelligence structure of the poem), that fuse into total form—a unifying function and result: from the plurality of various movements to the unity of a single fact, the continuum called the poem.

The internal form makes the external form rock-solid, instead of leaving the external form just an empty shell, by providing the back-up structure. The internal form is not made by the language nor by technique but by this internal architectonics in a poem.

Thus a good poem has: a horizontal construction or dimension of language and music and a vertical construction and dimension of theme and sense. It can be read horizontally for its structure as verse and pleasures and vertically for its intellectual structure and pleasures; the poem moves cohesively and vertically in height and depth.

### THE LAST LINE

As the poem progresses, the semantic force will continually accelerate until the end, but only then will the semantic force exceed and overpower both the musical force and the verbal force with an implosion of meaning.

Trying to nail a last line is like trying to catch a lizard without its tail falling off. Without a tail, the bad poet's poems have a quality of incompleteness and no impact.

**Figure 19.** Emily Dickinson's poem "Parting," in *Twentieth Century American Poetry*(10), is an illustration of an effective (imploded) last line:

*Parting*

My life closed twice before its close;
It yet remains to see
If Immortality unveil
A third event to me,

So huge, so hopeless to conceive,
As these that twice befell.
Parting is all we know of heaven,
And all we need of hell.

**Figure 20.** The following is an illustration drawn by Villa to show how the last line implodes the poem with meaning:

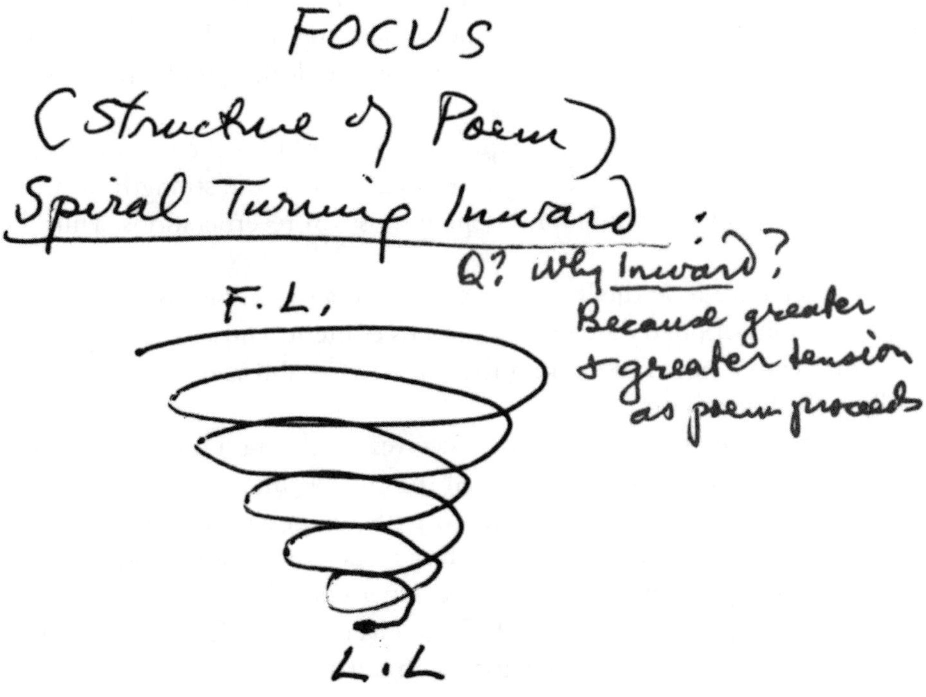

In the poem, the tension has become greater and greater as it progresses, and now demands closure—it cannot go much farther. The poem must end because the tension cannot bear it anymore, and not because you have nothing more to say. The technical solution of the poem and the thematic solution of the poem then have met in one lyric total.

It may happen that your intellectual form is finished when the exterior form remains unfinished in which case you have an unfinished pattern. Or the reverse (where you have a premature closure instead of a delayed closure). In both cases, the two forms have not come together, i.e., one still needs fulfillment. Therefore, you have a bad poem since in a good poem the internal force and the external force are coterminous and balanced and the poem stops in perfect time.

An artist knows when to stop. He or she knows when the poem is complete. He or she cannot afford to stop earlier or later. The last line is the poet's moment of insight where the quarry is caught. Before the last line, the other lines were only hidden resources until the last line reveals their riches. At the end of every good poem is a snap like the crack of a whip, which makes the poem read true.

### THE LYRIC TOTAL

Lyric totals—when they are found in art—are more than the sum of their parts. In art, whether it is prose or poetry, painting or sculpture—the total is more than the sum of its parts because we are dealing with an aesthetic art total.

In prose art, the prose total equals $C+r$, where $C$ is the content and $r$ its reverberations. In prose, $C$ is greater than its $r$, as the strength of prose resides mainly in its content and depends less on reverberations. Thus, in prose, $C > r$.

In poetry, we have the lyric total which equals $c+R$. This is because the reverberations of poetry are greater than its content. Thus, $R > c$ in poetry.

You begin a poem by pulling the top down—and you end a poem by pulling the bottom up.

When the poem ends, the poet receives, as through a sudden explosion, a moment of truth and insight. At the end, we may say the poem sews itself together. With the last line, which pulls the poem together and boomerangs the meaning of all the preceding lines—the meaning or outcome becomes the main event—and then you experience the complete poem.

Where the previous lines might have given you knife-thrusts, the last line gives you a knife-twist—not just a stab but a twist.

The poem flowers at its conclusion. The poet has been building the bud of his or her poem. Yet, at completion of the technical work the bud suddenly erupts into full florescence, into a full blossom of meaning where everything falls into place. This flowering is the bursting of this technically-perfect bud in a rose of poetic meaning. Now there is an explosion and a feedback happening.

The poem now has been shut and closed if you are working as an artist, with no other endings possible, nor with any other endings beyond. The closing is final and with authority.

The last line has locked the poem completely, into form and total meaning. It gives the right relief to the suspension, stretching and tension built up before. All previous lines are pivoted to the last line, although the poet himself could not have known it while he was writing the poem. While superficially it seems that the last line frames the poem, actually the last line is framed by the whole poem.

Where tension was only an implosive factor (an inward tightener), the last line is an explosive factor and explodes the poem to full bloom.

Poetry is a sequence, from an opening in delight to a resolution in insight. A poem must always reach insight.

Dylan Thomas: "The poem is, as all poems are, its own question and answer, its own contradiction, its own agreement.... The aim of the poem is the mark that the poem itself makes: it's the bullet and the bull's eye; the knife, the growth and the patient."

When you get to the last line, the time has arrived for you to deliver with full force whatever life-force, intelligence or spiritual force you have.

The circuit of the poem must be closed, and it is the final line that closes and locks this circuit.

As if by total recall, the last line remembers the first line and connects with it. The first line was a feel-*forward*, but the last line is now a feed*back*. The last line ricochets and zippers up the poem, so that it is not only complete but closed. The poem has coiled back upon itself. The circuitry has accomplished a retroactive impact and meaning to all preceding details so that now they bud out and connect to a simple vitality. A cyclic situation, a round-robin effect, is accomplished and now the poem is a continuum.

Valéry called Mallarmé's poems "little crystal systems." A "little crystal system" means a closed system or a completed circuit. The poem has a universe of its own, self-sufficient, autonomous and complete—a continuum.

The last line does not lead out but switches back to the first line—to wrap up the poem in neat bundle. The last line must be a master-stroke, for it wields the intellectual thrust of the poem.

The first line was not only a good place to take off from but, for the good poet, also a good place to return home. What grew from the first line closes in to contain itself at the end.

In the poetry of Dylan Thomas, the lines are pointed, but his poems are pointless. On the other hand, Emily Dickinson was a master poet in terms of the insight of her last lines.[41]

Effecting a circuitry is the sign of a master. But, if the last line fails to click, the circuit remains incomplete and the system lies open. You have only the interlineal and interstanzaic connections but the terminals, beginning to end, are unconnected. On the other hand, the circuited poem has traveled from A to Z and then back to A.

A poem must have impact—that is what the circuit effects.

Therefore, let us summarize the function of the last line:

1. It completes the technical structure and locks the exterior force.
2. It completes the content and locks it into intellectual force.
3. It fuses exterior force and intellectual force into one individual force.
4. It clicks the poem with a lyric total.

The versification is poetric. The build-up to climax is poeimic. The overall essence is poetic.

ROBERT FROST: You can't make a poem without a point.

The point is what gives bite to the poem. A poem must have bite. There are poems with lines that are pointed and have teeth—yet, the poem itself may be pointless. For example, Dylan Thomas is more convincing in his lines than in the totality of his poems. As George Steiner said: "There is less there than meets the dazzled eye." This is what happens with an uncircuited poem.

---

41 Since a good last line is indigenous to the poem that it closes, finding the right last line is a poem-by-poem task, and cannot be taught in the way that the technique of versification is taught in Chapter 23, or as Villa taught technique in his Poetry Workshop III sessions. There is one exception. In Chapter 23 and in the Appendix on Adaptations, we discuss Villa's use of adaptations to train his students in the technique of versification. The adaptation assignments were also of utility in learning to recognize where the (adapted) poem should begin *and end*, and thus were helpful in recognizing a good last line. Nailing the last line requires both the external poet and the internal poet (see Chapter 3), and the closest one can come to teaching the internal poet is to counsel him or her to live a good life.

Of William Carlos Williams, R.P. Blackmur said: "He is objectivism—without objective."

**Figure 21.** Villa used the following diagram to demonstrate where you can end your poem.

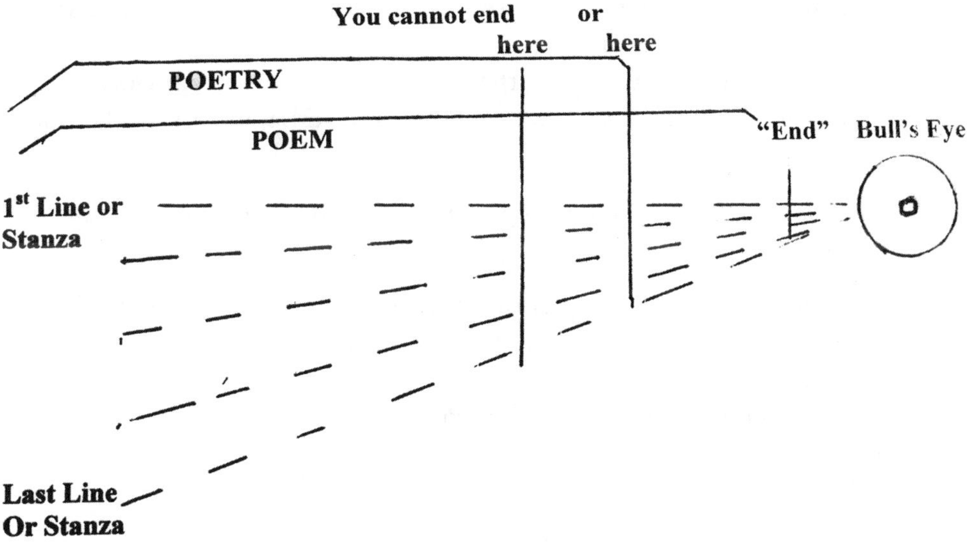


The bull's eye is, of course, the proper ending, where the poet should end the poem with finality, with his or her point. The poem then is fully closed. The areas designated as "here" and "here" are so distant from the proper ending that, if the poet ends there, the poet has only poetry but not a poem. If the poet chooses to end the poem at the "End," he or she may have a poem, although the poet did not hit the precise bull's eye. Why? Because, being very close to the bull's eye, the poet allows the point to be inferred. You have then what we may call an open ending rather than a closed ending. However, the poem is not shut tight. The poem may be more subtle perhaps, but also more obscure and you have less finality—what you may call a poem with indirect lighting.

### THE CREATION OF A POEM

Let us look back on what happens in the creation of a poem. The poem begins in silence—in a moment of poetic intuition. It begins non-verbal; there are no words yet. The poetic intuition is the first major thrust in the creation of the poem.

Next comes the first line, which of course is verbal. This is the second main thrust, as there is a build-up and key-up of tension and technique.

The third, but not yet final, major thrust, is the last line. The last line has stopped the poem, but has not actually ended it. There is a *beyond-wordness* to the poem, the poem's final major thrust. Although the words stop, the poem goes on—to reverberations, to a non-verbal silence. This is the part of the poem that the writer does not state but intuits to the reader. The final meaning of the poem is non-verbal because it is non-discursive. It cannot be discussed or explained.

And so we will end by saying that: A poem is a non-verbal work of art with a verbal body. Or, we may say: poetry is the verbal pursuit of the non-verbal.

> PAUL VALÉRY: "Poetry attempts by 'words' to create the condition of an absence of words."

Reverberations after completion of the last line are not a silence but a series of ripples or movements in silence—what we call the *beyond-wordness of poetry.*

George Steiner said: "Where the word of the poet ceases, a great light begins."

# Villa's Postscript

What this book has provided is the mental construction, through a coherent imagination, of what we may call the *archetype or model poem*, or the *critical model.* Having completed and understood the foregoing, you have reached an awkward stage—where you are now too knowledgeable to be called mere amateurs, and yet are not ready to be truly accomplished.

To catch on, you must study poetry more, not just enough but enough enough. You must reach the point where you are at one with technique. This takes a long time—learning the craft (technique) of art requires at least ten years.

**Figure 22.** Although this book has given you an awareness of technique, you are still not *at one* with it. The state of your evolution is as portrayed below:

The silence after the last line—the *beyond-wordness of poetry*—is meaningful—it is what speaks for the poem. Where the poem only sang before, now in silence it speaks its power. Its music is now a metaphysic. Its language is now a tranquility. Its content is now in our blood. The poem has moved from a poet's silence to its own silence and then to the ethic of the human heart.

It is a silence that has *authority*—ordinary silence lacks authority.

HONORÉ DE BALZAC: A man does not recognize as his own what he has written as a poet.

# Poetry is

# EDITOR'S EPILOGUE

Among the most-important messages conveyed by Villa's theory of poetry is his counsel in Chapter One: "After reading a poem, the question to ask is: 'How did the poet do it?'—not: 'What did he say?'"

Having now read Villa's theory, you can understand why he offered this counsel. In simplified terms, he did so because, as he also said: "A work of art is not what it is about, but what it actually is: its qualities of writing. These are what make us experience the art."

The latter statement, unless explained, has led to a great deal of confusion about Villa's theory. Villa is *not* saying that a poem that "says something" to the reader, even something meaningful, is a faulty poem for doing so. Indeed, Villa makes clear in Chapters 13 and 14 that "great poetry," that is, poems which are "God-like in [their] great humanism, or what we might call art for man's sake, or, alternatively, art for mind's sake," is at the top of the hierarchy of poetry. He places them above "great minor poetry," poems that are great simply by craft and sensory beauty because of their beauty of expression and form. The latter poems are "pure...in the sense of the chasteness of the art without the intrusion of any foreign matter."

Villa makes clear that, in terms of *ars poetica*, "meaning alone cannot make a work of art—it is always the form that accomplishes it." Thus, he says that a "poet" who begins a poem with the deliberate intention of "saying something" is not working by the poetic process, which "starts from the energy and self-kindling of language itself." Villa went so far as to say that when you begin a poem with a meaning in mind, that meaning—instead of building the poem up—undermines it, pulls it down and it has a birth defect.

Under Villa's theory, great poetry must generate itself from the verbal and musical development of the poem. "It must be a subconscious arrival by the poetic process." (70) In the great poem, the fineness and depth of the great poet's life and character have evoked and elicited a great meaning. The meaning was pulled out of the poet by the writing of the poem utilizing the poetic process.

As a consequence, Villa prescribed that: "We must not think of poetry as in the service of something else. We speak loosely of poetry as narrative poetry, satirical poetry, didactic poetry, dramatic poetry, but none of these is related to the art of poetry... They involve verse applied to the matter and uses of prose." (11)

It is ironic that the foregoing aspects of Villa's theory, intended by him to "focus clearly so that poetry no longer is the victim of *mistaken identity*," should lead to so much misperception of his theory or of his motives in formulating and propounding it. Across two cultures and two continents—in the Philippines, where Villa was born, and in his adopted country, the United States—Villa was confronted and berated based upon misunderstandings of his foregoing views on the function of meaning in poetry.

In the Philippines, Villa was a respected literary figure, a renowned literary critic, and designated "National Artist" by the Government, among other honors. However, during a visit to the Philippines in 1937, Villa was "berated" (Villa's term) by his friend, Salvador P. Lopez, also a prized Filipino literary figure, for being oblivious of the current issues of the day, stunted by his unconcern with the social disorder, and distancing himself from economic uncertainty and dearth. Lopez, who subsequently held many important positions, including President of the University of the Philippines, Secretary of Foreign Affairs and Ambassador to the United Nations, clung to these views even many years thereafter, declaring in a 1984 interview that he had done "the right thing" in chiding Villa for insisting on art for art's sake in rebutting Lopez's cry of art for Social Realism. (In 1937, Villa had countered Lopez's criticism by explaining that: "The reason for my unpoliticality is that I do not believe the economic readjustment of society to be the function of literature. And, although literature may record or reflect the social conditions of a time, literature does not exist for the mere recordance of it. A work of literature is not the more valid in that it records or contains a social upheaval—the validity of literature is dependent upon no such purely circumstantial event, but upon the revolution of the internal personality of man...Literature lives because it is the portrayal of the eternal human spirit, of the essences of things; it is the drama of the human soul and not the drama of the brokerage chart.")[42]

Although, in 1937, Villa was famous in the Philippines for his short stories, hence his prose, and although Villa took up serious poetry writing the following year after being influenced by reading the poems of E. E. Cummings in *Collected Poems by E. E. Cummings* (New York: Harcourt, Brace,

---

42 As reported in *The Critical Villa: Essays in Literary Critcism*, Jonathan Chua, ed. (Quezon City: Ateneo de Manila University Press, 2002), 178–79.

1938), Villa's views on literature did not change as witness his statements that poetry should not be thought of as in the service of something else and that didactic poetry is merely verse applied to the matter and uses of prose. Although in later years Lopez did not abandon his criticism of Villa, it is clear that his disagreement with Villa was not personal, as he described Villa as "the one Filipino writer today who it would be futile to deride and impossible to ignore."

On the American continent, however, the disputation of Villa's views on whether the primary function of poetry as art is to "say something" was different. There was no disagreement over whether the poet should take up the cause of proletarian literature (or propaganda as Villa labeled it), but disagreement over a "revolution" in American poetry proclaimed by a contemporary and acquaintance of Villa, Louis Simpson. When they first met in the early 1940s, both were at Columbia University studying under the tutelage of Mark Van Doren. Simpson was also an aspiring poet, and their paths crossed several times thereafter. In a March 1, 1992 article on the front page of *The New York Times Sunday Book Review*, Simpson complained that Villa—whom he referred to under the pseudonym "Neville Dane"—had criticized Simpson's poetry because: "I was trying to 'say' something." Derisively, he quoted Villa: "Poetry shouldn't be 'about' anything."

Simpson's article can only be described as a virulent attack on Villa's standing as a poet and a mocking of Villa's innovations in poetic technique. In context, it is clear that the motivation for Simpson's attack was jealousy of the acclaim Villa experienced upon his publications of his poems and Villa's above noted criticism of Simpson's own efforts.

In 1979, Simpson published a book, *A Revolution in Taste—Studies of Dylan Thomas, Allen Ginsberg, Sylvia Plath and Robert Lowell* (New York: Macmillan Publishing, 1978). There, Simpson proclaimed that the art of poetry had passed from the likes of Auden and Dylan Thomas to Allen Ginsberg and others (presumably including Simpson himself). The "revolution" was described by Simpson in the Foreword to his book as follows:

> The poet moved to the center of the stage and spoke his mind freely. This became the common stance for poets in the years that followed. "Most artists and critics," said Susan Sontag, writing in the sixties, "have discarded the theory of art as representation of an outer reality in favor of *art as subjective expression*." (Emphasis added.)

Unfortunately, Simpson's assessment of the direction that American poetry took in the 1960s is not far from the truth. Under the banner of a new freedom, poetry has strayed to the prosaic and the prosy, and the new "art as subjective expression" has purportedly liberated poets from the demands of versification and away from anything that smacks of "formalism," even the emphasis on *poetic language and form* that has made poetry an art.

While one can quarrel over the reasons, there can be no denial that over the past half century there has been a severe decline in general readership of poetry in America. As Dana Gioia observed,

> Over the past half century, as American poetry's specialist audience has steadily expanded, its general readership has declined. Moreover, the engines that have driven poetry's institutional success...have unwittingly contributed to its disappearance from public view.[43]

Jay Parini also wrote:

> "Most poetry written after the mid-twentieth century is 'free verse,' as anyone will know..."[44]

As Villa's theory makes evident, Villa shared with his good friend Cummings a belief in creating a modern lyrical form of poetry—letting form develop organically from the poetic language and differing from the formalism of the past in that neither insisted upon strict attention to metrics, adherence to arbitrary and fixed forms, requirement for imagery and insistence on rhyme. In a letter Villa wrote to Cummings describing a Guggenheim project he was to apply for in 1951 (and which ultimately produced Villa's theory), Villa wrote: "Although I would rather write poems instead, the project somehow pleases me for it is about *our kind of poetry, which is the True Poetry*—though everybody else be to the contrary..." (Emphasis added.)

Villa's theory of poetry, while not intended to be so, is in fact a manifesto to reverse the effects of Simpson's self-proclaimed "revolution" and to return American poetry to its rightful place as the art of writing lyric poetry of formal excellence.

In Villa's papers sorted by his Literary Trustee after Villa's death, was found a Simpson "poem" that, through adaptation Villa turned into a "diamond." (See the Appendix on Adaptations.) I commend that adaptation to you as a metaphor for what has led to the decline in general readership of American poetry in the past half century.

---

43 Dana Gioia, *Can Poetry Matter?*, 2 (Saint Paul: Graywolf Press, 10th Ann. Ed., 2002).

44 Jay Parini, *Why Poetry Matters*, xii (New Haven: Yale U. Press, 2008).

# APPENDIX ON ADAPTATIONS

Villa's guidelines to students for executing his adaptation assignments were:

<u>Concerning ASSIGNMENTS</u>

Our Assignments fall into two categories:

I. Those which are supposedly already in "verse," but which, unfortunately, are badly done.
(You get few of these because most poems published are so miserably written that they are irredeemable.)

II. Those which have to be <u>put</u> into verse -- <u>from prose</u>.
(Normally or abnormally this is <u>not</u> the creative process for poetry, but such assignments afford good training towards learning economy of means, and versification.
These assignments, therefore, require <u>editing</u>.
A poem so produced is called an <u>Adaptation</u>.)

<u>GUIDELINE NOTES for ADAPTATIONS</u>

In making <u>Adaptations</u>, please remember:

1) A <u>Title</u> can be used as an <u>integral part</u> of the poem, although the the title itself remains "outside" the poem's form.
(Cf. Marianne Moore's "The Fish")

2) You may <u>remove</u> words, phrases, clauses, even whole sentences, from anywhere in the text if you deem them inessential to the poem you are making.

3) However, you may NOT add words (except for poetic exclamations like 'O', 'oh', 'ah' -- which are for poetic intensification).

4) You may, however, <u>repeat</u> words or phrases which are in the text -- as a poetic device.

5) You may use <u>contractions</u> ("You're" for "You are", etc.)

6) You may change the <u>number</u> -- i.e., convert the plural to singular ("mankind" or "men" to "man", -- or vice-versa).

7) You may <u>invert</u> sentence structure, if it helps achieve better euphony.
(E.g.: "I like Arthur's attitude" may be altered to "Arthur's attitude I like.")

8) You may <u>change</u> the tense of a verb or of the poem itself if it will improve the poem.

9) Above all, do not maul the text. Stick to the <u>original sequence</u> of language, do not scramble it up -- UNLESS to the <u>benefit</u> of the poem.

10) Poems are not dogs and should have no tails (loose line at end, if it is unbalanced elsewhere. In this case, Note 1, above, might be useful as a device.)

11. You may capitalize or uncapitalize or italicize others to fit the sensibility of the work.

12. You may change the original punctuations or add new punctuations to suit the movement of the verse.

Found in Villa's papers after his death was his adaptation of the last two stanzas of Louis Simpson's nine-stanza poem "The People Next Door." (The entire poem is found in Simpson's book: *The Owner of the House—New Collected Poems 1940–2001* [Rochester: BOA Editions, 2003, 350–52].) However, I reproduce below just the last four stanzas so that the reader can see what was going on in the portion Villa adapted:

Yes, I believe in the family...
next door. I rejoice
at their incomings and outgoings.
I am present when Betty
goes out on her first date.
I hear about Joey's being chosen
for the team. I survive the takeover
of the business, and the bad scare
at the doctor's.
I laugh with them that laugh
and mourn with them that mourn

I see their lights, and hear a murmur
of voices from house to house.

It gives me a strange feeling
to think how far they've come
from some far world to this,
bending their necks to the yoke
of affection.

And that one day
with a few simple words
and flowers to keep them company
they'll return once more to the silence
out there, beyond the stars.

(It should be noted that the final three words, "beyond the stars," were not found in the copy of this poem from which Villa made his adaptation, and that their later addition by Simpson violates Villa's guideline 10 for making adaptations: "Poems are not dogs and should have no tails (loose line at end...)"

And so I present Villa's adaptation, which has the added virtue that Villa used one of his new innovative techniques—referred to by him as "duo-technique"—to facilitate the movement, tensions and suspensions of his adaptation.

How far
we've come

from some
far world! to this

Yoke of
Affection—

And one
day, with a few

simple
words and

flowers...
return to silence.

—JGV
Adapted from
Louis Simpson

(Readers interested in learning more about "duo technique" should refer to the Penguin Classics' 2008 publication of Villa's *Collected Poems* mentioned in footnote 32 on page 127 above. There duo-technique is explained and examples given at 227–39.)

As to the adaptation of prose matter to a poem, an example may demonstrate the value of the process in learning or practicing the technique of versification. The following is a (prose) *New York Times* theater review of a production of "Joyicity," a theatric celebration of the language of James Joyce:

Reviews/**Theater**

# *Getting to the Heart of Joyce With His Own Words*

By WILBORN HAMPTON

Whether jigging a jiggily jig down the Liffey or juggling a jangly jingle jiffily, there's joyance and jollity in "Joyicity." Ah, that Jimmy Joyce, he knew a bit of the lingo, by jingo.

All alliterative allusion aside, "Joyicity," an Abbey Theater production being presented by the Irish Repertory Theater, is an inspired hour based on the life and work of James Joyce, a celebration of language through the pen of perhaps our century's greatest master. The material has been judiciously selected and expertly woven together by Ulick O'Connor and is given an enlightened performance by Vincent O'Neill.

The show is basically a succinct yet insightful biography of Joyce told through recitation and enactment of passages from his works as well as anecdotal matter from Richard Ellmann's brilliant "James Joyce."

No prerequisite reading or homework is necessary. "Joyicity" can be a primer for anyone daunted by Joyce's reputation as an Olympian writer of incomprehensible gobbledygook, yet at the same time delight and entertain genuine Joyceans.

What emerges is a miniature portrait of the artist as a young, middle-aged and older man, all too human, searching for the same things we all want to know — Who are we? Where did we come from? Where are we going? — and finding the traditional answers unsatisfying.

**Joyicity**

Fergus Burke

Vincent O'Neill

By Ulick O'Connor; directed by Caroline FitzGerald; original music by Noel Eccles; set design by David Raphel; lighting by Gregory Cohen; production stage manager, Chris Kelly. Presented by the Irish Repertory Theater, Charlotte Moore and Ciaran O'Reilly, artistic directors, and One World Foundation. At Actors' Playhouse, 100 Seventh Avenue South, at Christopher Street, Greenwich Village.

WITH: Vincent O'Neill.

•

Appropriately, "Joyicity" begins on the banks of the river Liffey in the English-ruled, Catholic-confessed Dublin where Joyce was bred-and-buttered. There are his alcoholic father and long-suffering mother, who bore 15 children, and his brother Stanislaus, his lifelong critic and friend. And there is his walk down Nassau Street in June 1904, when he first saw Nora Barnacle, the woman who became his wife and muse and would stick with him through thick and thin ("Barnacle by name, barnacle by nature").

Although Joyce soon turns his back on both King and Pope and flees to Paris, Trieste, Zurich and points in between, he can leave neither family nor Dublin nor the Liffey completely behind. As Ellmann pointed out, if Joyce sought to fly past the net of his family, his life's works were all entangled in it.

Mr. O'Connor whisks us along on Joyce's Odyssean exile, pointing out the literary landmarks on the way, while the artist metamorphoses from the witty darling of Dublin's musical evenings into a monkish expatriate, an international literatus sneaking off from Nora to cadge a bottle of wine from the men's room attendant at his regular Paris bistro.

In weaving this delicate tapestry, Mr. O'Connor has interlaced some of Joyce's early love poetry with lines from "Pomes Penyeach" and even the odd limerick. Scenes from "Ulysses" and "Finnegans Wake" have been deftly edited and seamlessly stitched together and reflect a broader appreciation of the canon than more predictable selections like Molly Bloom's reverie or the final paragraph of "The Dead." Through it all, Mr. O'Connor has kept the conjunctive matter at a minimum and left most of the talking to Joyce.

The adroitness of the text is matched by a masterly reading from Mr. O'Neill. To confront the words alone must be terrifying. One dropped syllable and the whole poetic cadence is lost. Not only does Mr. O'Neill bring them trippingly off the tongue; he also captures the affectionate irreverence with which they were first sent forth.

•

In the scene in Barney Kiernan's pub, from the Cyclops section of "Ulysses," Mr. O'Neill delivers a small tour de force. Playing the entire congregation — Bloom, citizen Joe, Little Alf, John Wyse, Terry Lenehen, J. J. — Mr. O'Neill switches voices, intonations and attitudes with such dexterity one can imagine a dozen actors on stage and even a real dog growling the part of Garryowen.

One could quibble about technique here and there. One might wish, for example, that Mr. O'Neill would take a bit more time with the final page from "Finnegans Wake" at the end or curtail his occasional tendencies to excessive gesturing.

But portraying a cast, both real and imagined, as rich as any in modern literature — from Gerty McDowell, who leans back to watch the fireworks and watch herself being watched, to the Ondt and Gracehopper fable in "Finnegans Wake" — Mr. O'Neill displays a keen understanding of his characters and material and carries his audience along with him.

Students in Villa's workshops were regularly assigned the task of identifying poetic material within prose material such as this and versifying same, keeping in mind Villa's guidelines. Frequently, as happened here, Villa's own execution of his assignment was superior to anything the students produced. However, even so, his students—having wrestled with the challenge—formed an appreciation of the demands (and rewards) of elevating their technique. In rare instances, a student came up with a rendition Villa recognized as superior to his own, whereupon Villa did not hesitate to acknowledge and lavish praise upon the feat. I say "rare instances" because I can recall only two instances in my more than 25 years of studying with Villa in which my own versions were accepted as the defining ones.

At any rate, the foregoing assignment was not one of them, and you can see from the adaptation by Villa that follows why Villa's execution trumped all contenders:

THE HEART OF JOYCE
(With His Own Words)

Whether
jigging a jiggily jig down
the Liffey . . .
or juggling

a jangly
jingle jiffily — there's joyance
and jollity in
"Joyicity!"

Ah, that
Jimmy Joyce he knew, a bit
of the lingo,
by jingo!

—Adaptation
by
Xocé. Xavie Villa

# BIBLIOGRAPHY

Aiken, Conrad, ed. *Twentieth Century American Poetry*. New York: Modern Library Edition, Random House, 1963.

Auden, W. H., et al. *Poets at Work*. New York: Harcourt, Brace, Jovanovich, 1948.

Compton, Nancy. *Writers: Photographs*. New York: W. W. Norton, 2005.

Cummings, E. E., *Complete Poems, 1904–1962*, edited by George J. Firmage. New York: Liveright Publishing, 1991.

——. *A Miscellany*, edited by George J. Firmage. New York: The Argophile Press, 1958.

——. *Collected Poems*. New York: Harcourt, Brace, 1938.

Felstiner, John. *Can Poetry Save the Earth? A Field Guide to Nature Poems*. New Haven: Yale University Press, 2009

Frost, Robert. *The Poetry of Robert Frost: All eleven of his books-complete*. New York: Holt, Rinehart and Winston, 1969.

Gioia, Dana. *Can Poetry Matter? Essays on Poetry and American Culture*. 10th Anniversary Edition. Saint Paul: Graywolf Press, 2002.

Greenberg, Clement. "Modernist Painting." In *The New Art: A Critical Anthology*, edited by Gregory Battcock. New York: Dutton, 1966.

Moore, Marianne. *The Complete Poems*. New York: Viking Press, 1967.

Parini, Jay. *Why Poetry Matters*. New Haven: Yale University Press, 2008.

Rizzo, Sergio. "Remembering Race: Extra-poetical Contexts and the Racial Other in 'The Red Wheelbarrow.'" *Journal of Modern Literature* 29, no. 1 (2005).

Simpson, Louis. *A Revolution in Taste: Studies of Dylan Thomas, Allen Ginsberg, Sylvia Plath and Robert Lowell*, New York: Macmillan Publishing, 1978.

——. *The Owner of the House: New Collected Poems 1940–2001*. Rochester: BOA Editions, 2003.

Valéry, Paul. *Aesthetics* [Bollingen Series XLV, 13], translated by Ralph Manheim, and edited by Jackson Mathews. Princeton: Princeton University Press, 1964.

——. *The Art of Poetry,* [Bollingen Series XLV, 7], translated by Denise Folliot, and edited by Jackson Mathews. Princeton: Princeton University Press, 1958.

——. *Selected Writings*. Various translators. New York: New Directions, 1950.

Villa, Jose Garcia. *Have Come, Am Here*. New York: Viking Press, 1942.

——. *José Garcia Villa—Doveglion* (pseud.): *Collected Poems*, edited by John Edwin Cowen. New York: Penguin Group, 2008.

——. *Selected poems and new*. New York: McDowell, Obolensky, 1958.

Williams, Oscar, ed. *A Pocket Book of Modern Verse.* New York: Washington Square Press, Simon & Schuster, 1958.

# INDEX


## A

Abstraction, 35, 39, 57–61, 143-47

Adaptations, xii, 127, 152, 162–67

Agee, James, 25

Adjectives for poetry, The, 90–91, 152

Aiken, Conrad, 5, 22

Amrau, David, 22

Anderson, Sherwood, 43

Appolinaire, Guillaume, 13

Auden, W. H., x, xii, xv, 4, 8, 13, 15–16, 21–22, 66, 69, 73, 112, 118, 161

## B

Balzac, Honoré de, 23, 156

Barker, George, 5, 53, 66, 70, 121

Barthes, Roland, 118

Bell, Clive, 64

Beyond-wordness of poetry, The, 154, 156

Bishop, Elizabeth, x, 49

Bishop, John Peale, 47

Blackmur, R.P., 48, 111, 118, 141, 153

Blake, William, 92, 117

Borderline cases, 42-44

Bowen, Elizabeth, 26

Bracque, Georges, 86, 90

Bravo magazine, xiii–xvi

Browning, Elizabeth Barrett, 92

Burden, Jean, 23

Burnshaw, Stanley, 112

## C

Calas, Nicolas, 60

Calisher, Hortense, 19, 86

Campion, Thomas, 121

Capote, Truman, 43

Carroll, Lewis, xi, 58

Chekhov, Anton, 20

Ciardi, John, 97, 116

Clarke, Austin, 87

Cocteau, Jean, 90, 93, 102

Coleridge, Samuel Taylor, 61, 73, 91

Cowen, John Edwin, ix, xiii, xvi, 127

Crane, Stephen, 47

Creative Expression, 8–9, 77, 79

Cronin, A.J., 20

Cummings, E. E., xi–xii, 4–5, 22, 28, 43, 47, 52–53, 58, 78, 81–84, 86, 89, 91–92, 99, 103, 121, 127, 141, 160, 162

**D**

de Banville, Theodore, 116

Degas, Edgar, 24

Denwood, Jon, 99

Dickinson, Emily, 5, 54, 74, 91, 99–100, 103, 116, 141, 149, 152

Diderot, Denis, 89

Donne, John, 73, 82, 91, 103, 121

Don'ts of the Art of Poetry, The, 100–2

Dryden, John, 113

**E**

Eberhart, Richard, x, 5, 22, 40, 69, 74, 78, 91, 97, 112, 121, 141, 143

Eliot, T.S., 9, 21, 37, 40, 46, 50, 64, 73, 94–95, 98, 123

**F**

Faulkner, William, 89

Fixed forms, 1–2, 162

Flaubert, Gustave, 62

Forster, E.M., 22

Free verse, xi, xv–xvi, 1, 43, 45–49, 90, 130, 135, 162

Frost, Robert, xi, xvi, 4, 5, 14–15, 19, 21, 25, 42, 46, 51–52, 60, 73, 83, 87, 109–10, 112, 120–21, 125, 127, 141–42, 152

Fry, Christopher, 15–16

**G**

Gass, William, 110

Genesis in poetry, 20–23, 39

Gide, André, 52, 86–87

Gilson, Etienne, 62, 94

Gioia, Dana, 162

Goethe, Johann Wolfgang von, 27, 87

Graves, Robert, 119

Great poetry, 3, 56–57, 68–74, 121–22, 159

Greenberg, Clement, 60

Guerard, Albert, 59

Guy, Gloria, 131–33, 137–38

**H**

Hardy, Thomas, 3

Heath-Stubbs, John, 54

Herbert, George, 121

Herrick, Robert, 121

Hopkins, Gerard Manley, 5, 38, 73-74, 82, 91–92, 99, 103, 121, 127

Houghton Library Collection, ix, xiv, xix

Housman, A.E., 66

**I**

Imagery, 1–2, 45, 49, 66, 82, 95, 99, 162

Inception of a poem, The, 93–103

**J**

Joyce, James, 17, 43, 58, 165–67

### K

Kafka, Franz, 13, 86

Kant, Immanuel, 62

Keats, John, 73, 92

Kinetics of poetry, 24–25, 39

### L

Language of poetry, The, 26–29, 36, 79, 80–83, 86–87, 101, 115–19, 139–40, 162

Last line, The, xi–xii, 18, 33, 98, 139–40, 148–54, 156

Line structure, 33-35, 45–46, 124–31, 135–40

Lopez, Salvador P., 160–61

Lowell, Amy, 47

Lyrical poetry, xiv–xv, xvii, 11, 32, 50–54, 56, 69–71, 73, 80, 88–89, 91, 110, 124, 131, 139–40, 145, 162

Lyrical spirit, 11, 13–14, 50–54, 90

### M

MacLeish, Archibald, 21, 22, 112

Magic in poetry, 19–20, 23, 29, 39, 52–54, 56–57, 64, 68–70, 81, 99, 139–40

Mallarmé, Stéphane, 24, 37, 93, 111, 151

Mann, Thomas, 43, 56

Maritain, Jacques, 64, 67, 89, 95, 123

Matisse, Henri, 9

McCarthy, Mary, 25

McLuhan, Marshall, 39, 77, 81, 87

Meaning in poetry, xvii, 3–4, 6, 17–18, 20–22, 24–26, 37–38, 41, 53, 55, 69–71, 76–78, 120–23, 159–60

Meredith, William, 30

Metaphors, xi, 35–37, 49, 80, 99, 101, 117, 144–47

Metrics, 1–2, 30–31, 45, 162

Mitchell, Margaret, 20

Moore, George, 64

Moore, Marianne, x, xi, 33, 41, 47, 51, 85, 91–92, 107, 127–30, 143

Morley, Christopher, 22

Movement of the poetic line, 107, 127–32, 135–37

Musical line of force, The, 104–6, 109–14

### N

Nabokov, Vladimir, 146

Nash, Ogden, 43, 63–64

Nemerov, Howard, 93

Nietzsche, Friedrich, 74

### O

Owen, Wilfred, 5, 74, 121, 141

### P

Parini, Jay, 162

Perse, St. John, 85

Picasso, Pablo, 9, 145

Pivot words, 130–33, 135

Poe, Edgar Allan, 35

Poetic process, xvii, xx, 3, 9, 18, 20–25, 37, 40, 42, 48–49, 51–52, 70, 75, 85, 89–91, 97–98, 111, 120–21, 125, 132, 159

Poetic tension, 134, 139–40

Poetry and prose, differences, xv, xvii, 3-5, 10-11, 14, 17–44, 46, 78, 80–83, 100–1, 114, 118–19, 124–25, 136, 145, 150, 159–60

Poetry as art, 11, 14, 161

Poetry as spirit, 13, 14, 26, 43–44, 70, 73

Poetry Workshops I, II, and III, xi–xv, 1, 7, 12, 74, 127, 152, 163–67

Porter, Katherine Anne, 20

Pound, Ezra, 35, 47, 54, 98

Principles behind poetry, xii–xiii, xvi–xvii, xx, 10, 12, 18, 45, 49, 52, 68, 74, 90

Propulsion of the first line, xi, 98, 104–08

Purity in poetry, 23, 28, 55–70, 72–73, 120, 144

**R**

Ransom, John Crowe, 5, 47, 60, 121–22

Read, Sir Herbert, 4

Reinhardt, Ad, 60

Renard, Jules, 93

Resistances in crafting poems, 86–89, 107, 122, 125–26, 132, 141

Reverdy, Pierre, 16

Rhyme, xvi, 87, 140–42, 162

Rhythm in poetry, 2, 13, 16, 21, 28–31, 39, 47–48, 86–87, 94–95, 105, 109, 113–17, 122, 125–26, 130, 132, 139

Riddell, Alan, 65–66

Riding, Laura, 4, 144

Rorem, Ned, 3, 22, 32, 76, 112

Rosenberg, Harold, 57

**S**

Sandburg, Carl, 47

Santayana, George, 15

Schwartz, Delmore, x, 66

Semantic line of force, The, 105–6, 109, 113–14, 120–24, 148

Shakespeare, William, 11, 67, 79

Shapiro, Karl, 51

Shaw, George Bernard, 64

Shelley, Percy Bysshe, 92

Simpson, Louis, 161–62, 164–65

Sitwell, Dame Edith, x, xi, 5, 22, 51, 74, 89, 112

Spark, Muriel, 114

Spectrum of poetry, 55–57, 68, 72, 144

Spender, Stephen, x, 21, 50

Spirit of play, The, 53–54, 83, 102, 118

Stanzation, 41, 46, 106–7, 125, 129, 131–41, 143

Steinbeck, John, 43

Steiner, George, 109–10, 152, 154

Stein, Gertrude, 45, 48–49, 53, 58, 62, 76, 78, 83, 115, 120, 144–45

Stein, Leo, 144

Stevens, Wallace, 3, 5, 13, 15, 37, 47, 66, 82–83, 91–92, 103, 109, 120, 144–45

Swinburne, Algernon Charles, 119

**T**

Tennyson, Alfred Lord, 92

Theory of poetry, xi, xiv, xvii, xix–xxi, 1, 3, 11–12, 85, 159–60, 162

Thomas, Dylan, ix, xi, 2, 4–5, 12, 16–17, 26, 53–54, 66, 70, 79, 80, 82, 89, 91–92, 99, 103, 109, 115, 119, 121, 124, 140, 151–52, 161

Tolstoy, Leo, 73

Troy, William, 18

**V**

Valéry, Paul, xxi, 1, 2, 6–8, 14, 18, 21, 38, 53, 62, 95, 97, 100, 107, 110, 114, 123, 128, 142, 145–46, 151, 154

Van Doren, Mark, 22, 161

Verbal line of force, The, 105-6, 115-19

Versification, xi-xiii, xvii, 7, 14, 33–35, 39, 43, 45-50, 52, 69, 86, 91, 105–7, 112, 115, 124–46, 152, 161, 165

Villa, José Garcia, x and passim.

**W**

Wagner, George, 52, 119

Wagner, Richard, 51

Wheelock, John Hall, 89, 94

Whistler, John McNeill, 90

Whitman, Walt, 45, 48–49, 74, 102–3

Wilbur, Richard, 47, 107, 141–42

Wilde, Oscar, 37, 43, 57

Williams, Oscar, 5

Williams, William Carlos 45, 48–49, 141, 153

Wodehouse, P.J., 94

Wolfe, Thomas, 17, 19, 43, 89

Woolf, Virginia, 17, 19, 79

Wordsworth, William, 18, 73, 92

Wylie, Eleanor, 103

**Z**

Zukofsky, Louis, 112